THE
BUSINESS
GAME PLAN

THE
BUSINESS
GAME PLAN

What Former Athletes Need To Know
To Start, Grow And Sell a Business

JONATHAN MILLER

JONES MEDIA
PUBLISHING

The Business Game Plan : What Former Athletes Need To Know To Start, Grow, And Sell A Business

Jones Media Publishing
10645 N. Tatum Blvd. Ste. 200-166
Phoenix, AZ 85028
JonesMediaPublishing.com

Disclaimer:

The author strives to be as accurate and complete as possible in the creation of this book, notwithstanding the fact that the author does not warrant or represent at any time that the contents within are accurate due to the rapidly changing nature of the Internet. While all attempts have been made to verify information provided in this publication, the Author and the Publisher assume no responsibility and are not liable for errors, omissions, or contrary interpretation of the subject matter herein. The Author and Publisher hereby disclaim any liability, loss or damage incurred as a result of the application and utilization, whether directly or indirectly, of any information, suggestion, advice, or procedure in this book. Any perceived slights of specific persons, peoples, or organizations are unintentional.

In practical advice books, like anything else in life, there are no guarantees of income made. Readers are cautioned to rely on their own judgment about their individual circumstances to act accordingly. Readers are responsible for their own actions, choices, and results. This book is not intended for use as a source of legal, business, accounting or financial advice. All readers are advised to seek the services of competent professionals in legal, business, accounting, and finance field.

Printed in the United States of America

ISBN: 978-1-948382-90-8 paperback

TABLE OF CONTENTS

CHAPTER 1

EXITING PRO ATHLETICS

Many young children dream of becoming a professional athlete. That is *their dream and the one* dream they pursue. In many rare occasions, some achieve that goal. For those who do actually achieve a career as a professional athlete, what comes after their professional sports career is just as important as the one on the field. Often, when athletes complete their professional athletic careers, they may have already created a vision of what they want to do *next*. They may have an *idea* of where they want to go, but have no idea how to get there.

The good news is that, as a former pro athlete, you already have plenty of skills in your back pocket, and even better, you are highly sought after for your unique set of skills. You are goal-oriented, you know how to execute a game plan, and you're driven to succeed.

Remember that you have a lot of support, but it is up to you to seek out the help. In most professional sports there is a strong alumni bond. Some of the leagues have set up trusts and foundations to support and help the transition. The NFL has programs where the league will pay for some of an athlete's education. Once eligible, the NFL will reimburse 100% of tuition up to $10,000 per calendar year for job-related education and training. This is a great chance to pursue a new career or pick up one that you may have left behind after joining the league. Considering a career in sales? Use this tuition reimbursement to pursue an MBA. If it makes sense for your career goals, why not?

For example, depending on what you want to do, a Master's in Business Administration (MBA) is quite an accomplishment to achieve and will definitely help with furthering your career. An MBA is an excellent stepping stone to see what your post career options may be.

Regardless of whether it *is* an MBA or whether it is deciding to go to medical school, law school or any other secondary education, achieving that goal has great advantages. No matter what, there might be some additional education that you might need to get in order to keep moving down the path of where you want to go after your athletic career.

What do I want to do?
How do I know it's the right thing for me?
How do I get down the path once I choose what I want to do?

The most difficult part of the Post Career process is to figure out *what you want to do and HOW to you know if it is the right thing for you?* Education options are seemingly endless, however going back to school at age 30 or 40 can be very difficult and overwhelming after years of a set schedule and being comfortable in your daily life. School may be the last thing you want to think about.

No matter how long your professional career lasts, as discussed in other chapters, it will take 3 years to transition out of athletics and into the "real world." If your professional career was only a few years, there is still some additional level of education that you might want to consider.

Following a successful career, you have to consider what you *want* to do; how does it fit with your current lifestyle, family, interests. The process of considering what you're going to do requires help from others. Family, friends, mentors and your current team of advisors are great resources to help you figure it all out.

Who do I know?
How can they help?
How do I ask?

In my prior books, we spoke about the importance of networking. Now we come back to the results of the networking you did when you were playing.

Networking and meeting the people who you need to meet is crucially important to your ongoing success. Consider the many people you've met over the course of your career. Who can you help? Who can help you? Perhaps you know others who are just starting or coming out of college. If you are exiting a professional career, you may have had a three-year career, a five-year career, or a ten-year career.

NOW it's time to start making those calls.

Sometimes, it's not who you know directly, but asking the people in your current circle of influence, whom do *they* know. You may have five or ten contacts that you have collected over your life who are professionals in a specific industry. Don't forget that they also know other professionals. *That's* the importance of networking. It's impossible to know everyone directly yourself, but the chances of you knowing someone else with a connection is greater with every person you meet.

No matter where you are in your life or professional career, it is so important to collect those names now and keep in touch with those people. Whether you just connect with each other on Instagram or other forms of social media, or it's someone you send an email to every once in a while, don't let your connections collect dust! The important thing is not just to have a bunch of names in your contact list, but to *build* those relationships with people and take the time to call them in the off-season. People are often more eager to help than you may think. Simply ask, *Hey, can I shoot something by you? Can I ask you a question?*

We talk about having a Mentor in Chapter 3. Don't forget when you're starting out in any profession, having a mentor is an excellent idea. If you already have a mentor, great, if not, start looking around for someone who might be a great resource for you and where you want to go.

What type of Job or Career do I want?

Do I want to work for someone else?
Do I want to work for myself?

In making this decision for what you want to do next, look at your first two options:

Working for somebody else, or working for Yourself

Working for Yourself

Being your own boss is a completely different world from what you may have been used to as an athlete. You have a lot of choices and options when you work for yourself including being able to pick your own hours, how hard you want to work, how much money you want to make etc. You control your own destiny.

Working for yourself may mean owning your own business.

The next question you may ask is "*What type of business do I want to own?*"

Some industries/job choices include:

- Retail
- Independent Insurance agent
- Financial Advisors
- Real Estate
- Traditional professional services (CPA, Attorney, Doctor)

You will need to have a better understanding of each one and what it requires.

Retail businesses are open on Saturday, Sundays, and many evenings, even if you are not. Your employees will be there working. Some businesses are ONLY open in the evenings like a restaurant. There are a host of variables you have to consider when going through this process.

In making these decisions, you have to ask yourself questions to help you determine where you will excel. If you're not a morning person, you're not going to be an investment advisor because you'll need to be up early with the markets. If you don't want to be bothered with work on the weekends, retail may not work as you don't want to get a call at two o'clock on a Sunday that the air conditioning broke at your store.

What are some of the things to consider when thinking of starting a business regarding the time devoted or the lifestyle or education requirements?

You have to look at the *lifestyle* of a business owner in the industry you're considering. For example, *what kind of lifestyle does a real estate agent have? What kind of lifestyle does an investment advisor have? What kind of lifestyle does a CPA have?*

There are *so* many things to consider.
What am I going to do?
Where is my job going to be?
Where is my business going to be? AND
What kind of training or education does it take to get there?
Are you willing to make any necessary sacrifices to get to the next place?

Working for Someone Else

Getting a regular job as an employee has many options as well. As an employee you may have benefits such as health insurance, retirement, paid vacation and the security of a regular paycheck.

Additionally, you also have to consider requirements of travel, location of an office, do you have a commute, do you work from home, can you be transferred, is there growth in the business etc. Do you *want* to travel and be on the roads for weeks or months out of the year? Do you want weekends home? Will you have a job where you go to an office and a desk each day? Will you be around other people? Do you *want* to be around other people or work more independently?

It's time to start having those conversations now. Hopefully this is not something you're going to do right off the bat. First, you are going to read this book. These are *tough* decisions that you want to make with your family and loved ones as well. The sooner that you start thinking about your next steps, the easier everything will fall into place when the time is right.

CHAPTER 2

GOING PRO

The moment when you become an ex-athlete? If you are reading this book after your athletic career has come to an end, that moment is NOW. If you are reading this book during your collegiate or professional career, CONGRATULATIONS, you are already ahead of the game.

In my previous books, I mentioned the transition from "athlete" to "civilian" life. The dictionary defines transition as "a process or period in which something undergoes a change and passes from one state, stage, form, or activity to another." You will eventually undergo a change from being an athlete to your next "pro" career.

Transition – change – can sometimes be difficult for anybody who's been doing the same thing for a number of years. What we do for much of our lives can define us and who we are. You meet someone at a party, and you say, "Glad to meet you. What do you do?" "Oh," they may reply, "I'm a Doctor." Or "I'm a Police officer." Or "I'm a teacher." We closely identify ourselves with our professions. Our professions become part of us, and when we undergo a change from our professions, many times it feels as if our inner selves change also. Irrationally, we may feel like a shell of our former selves.

You may be at the crossroads for any number of reasons

- Injury
- Released from a team
- Unsigned as a Free Agent
- Voluntary retirement after a short or long successful career

If transition comes abruptly, the process is no different than being fired from any job. Getting fired happens quickly and no matter how well prepared you are, (or even how much you say "I hate this job, I wish they would fire me,)" it can be a stunner.

As an athlete, you may know that your athletic career is coming to a close at some point. At that point you must have a plan in place. You want to have your backup plan ready to go when the change happens, whether that change is abrupt and unexpected or whether you play to the end of a long career.

This is a good time for a reminder of what Taylor Pak said in her book "Fit for Business,"

"It's fair to say that the recruiting process is equitable to the job search, which means that ... athletes already have a great deal of practice. Finding the right home for your unique personality and skill set is not an easy task. It takes research (again lots of research) and some time to figure out what your strengths and weaknesses are."

Transitioning from athlete to civilian life takes an average of THREE YEARS.

Whether collegiate or professional, this is all you have done since you were a young child. Those three years are when most FINANCIAL and EMOTIONAL problems occur. ESPN and Sports Illustrated provided statistics that 78% of former professional athletes ran into financial issues during those first three years. Usually, those problems and issues arise because the athlete did not have a financial plan already in place before his or her transition happened. Even if you have a plan in place, adjusting to your new civilian life can be difficult. Suddenly your schedule is not what it had been for years. Suddenly your life is no longer scheduled for you. You are now 100% in control of your life, and that's not something most athletes are used to.

I have spoken to many former professional athletes regarding their transition experience and I found a common thread for all athletes. (This is very similar going from Military to Civilian life)

1. Year ONE is when most have discussed how the first year is taken up by merely adjusting to the fact they are no longer on a team, for some it was still training to get "back in the game" or waiting for the call that did not come.

2. Year TWO is spent in evaluating their options, finishing school if they did not have their degree and investigating potential jobs.

3. Year THREE is spent executing the plan.

This chapter is about developing THE PLAN. Your goal is to understand how to psychologically prepare yourself for when your athletic career ends before it ends. That can be a tough challenge for any athlete because you are expected to train to be the best possible. It's a challenge to think about life after sport because you have to concentrate on practice every day and prepare for game day. Somehow you must learn to balance your concentration on your present career with your consideration of your future one.

My interviews have a common response. There WILL come a time when there is no one telling you to get up, where to be, when to be where, when practice is, when dinner is, when and where the meeting is, and telling you it's lights out, "bed check." Basically, someone else has scheduled your life as an athlete for ten, fifteen, or more years. The point most former athletes make is that if you think it's hard being on a schedule, it's harder not to be. Adjusting to life without restrictions can be as hard as adjusting to strict ones, and you must be mentally prepared to understand your life will be very different when your athletic career ends.

As a highly performing athlete, you probably have been "playing your game" for a long time, perhaps since you were eight or ten years old. As a child, adults "scheduled" your life at home and at school. In college you had to follow a schedule of classes and your team's schedule. As an athlete, you also are following your coach's and your team's rigid schedule. When your athletic career is over, there is no one to schedule your life but you. You are free. You don't have to maintain a schedule if you don't want to. You can stay out all night and sleep all day. Many times, this is when depression will hit former athletes. To follow a schedule means you are more in control of your life than if you do not follow a schedule.

Unless you have a transition plan in place for your life, when you come to the end of your athletic career, you come to your "What do I do now?" moment. If you are in your 20's or 30's, your "What do I do now?" question is a question of "What do I do for the next 40 or 50 years?"

I want you to start using the tools and advantages you have as an athlete to do what we talked about in my other books. Build your brand. Network. Investigate and ask questions. You may not find the answer now, but you will have a good head start.

What profession would you like to be in? Once you decide, start moving in the direction of where you want to go. For example, if you would like to be in broadcasting, did you already begin making acquaintances, network, take workshops, or intern with a network. This goes back to networking. Network with as many people as you can in whatever profession you are interested in for when your athletic career is done.

Now is the time to develop a personal "mission statement". Whatever it is you want to do after your athletic career, whatever it is you want to be, it is good to know and understand YOUR personal mission. Start planning now. Set your goals. That's what a mission statement is. It's setting and defining your goals you want to attain.

What type of industries interest you? Research and use your network of people to find resources in those industries. Perhaps in the offseason volunteer as an intern to do work in something that interests you. Volunteering is a great foot-in-the- door strategy.

What is it that you want to accomplish? What is it you want to leave behind as your legacy? What are your core values? Your personal mission statement helps guide you in the direction you want to go. It helps you to think more deeply about your life, clarify your purpose, and identify what is truly important to you.

Why do you need a personal mission statement? To determine the direction in which you want to go. Writing a mission statement is an act of self- discovery. Some examples of personal mission statements are:

- Oprah Winfrey – "To be a teacher. And to be known for inspiring my students to be more than they thought they could be."
- Richard Branson, multi-millionaire founder of The Virgin Group – "To have fun in my journey through life and learn from my mistakes."

- Denise Morrison, CEO of Campbell Soup Company – "To serve as a leader, live a balanced life, and apply ethical principles to make a significant difference."

Don't forget COMPANIES have mission statements as well

- Microsoft – "Our mission is to empower every person and every organization on the planet to achieve more."
- Google – "To organize the world's information and make it universally accessible and useful."

Even universities have one

- The Clemson University Department of Athletics strives to be an elite Division I institution in providing support to all areas of the student-athlete experience.

Five questions to ask yourself in crafting your personal mission statement are:

- What is important and valuable to me?
- Where do I want to go in my life?
- What does "the best" look like to me?
- How do I want people to describe me?
- What kind of legacy do I want to leave behind?

Keep your statement short. Remember your statement is just as much about the people you want to impact as it is about yourself. Share your statement with trusted friends and family who might provide you with valuable insights about yourself and your statement. Don't be afraid to make changes, because as you grow and evolve, your mission may also. As a successful professional athlete, you have an opportunity to give back to your community. Perhaps that idea could be part of your mission statement as well.

When you consider what your mission statement will be, there is an acronym or abbreviation that may help you. It is S.M.A.R.T. You want a "smart" statement. Those letters stand for:

S – Specific. Be specific in stating your goals.

M –Measurable. Set limits to your goals. Make them something you can do.

A – Achievable. Make your goals something you can achieve.

R – Relevant. Make your goals logical to you.

T – Time Bound. Set a target date to reach your goal. Making your goals "Time Bound" sets a timeline to prevent procrastination.

Finally, what skills do you have that can help you in your transition to your new life? What is your personality? How have you gotten along with your teammates, front office staff, and coaches? How do you handle wins and losses? Possibly one of the best skills you can develop while a professional athlete is the skill of handling adversity.

In her book Fit for Business, Taylor Pak discusses that during most of your athletic career you have been gaining all the necessary experiences to develop a skill set that is perfect for the business world. "Athletes are capable professionals that all have the key qualities to succeed in life. By the time their ... sports careers are over, athletes will have spent countless hours training and investing their time in a sport that, up until this point, has very much defined their existence." She goes on to say that her entire life had been about her identity as an athlete. She states that what she "learned during the game" prepared her for life "after the game".

Taylor and Ogilvie (1984) in the Journal of Applied Sports Psychology, introduced the conceptual model of transition. The Society for Sport, Exercise and Performance Psychology newsletter issue from May 2016 talks about TRANSFERRABLE SKILLS that include the ability to perform under pressure, problem solving, organizational skills, ability to meet deadlines and challenges, setting and achieving goals, dedication, self-motivation and team related interpersonal skills.

Floyd Little, NFL Hall of Famer, says that all ... athletes have the keys to success, and they are Drive, Determination, Dedication, Desire, Commitment and Sacrifice.

For example, losing a big game by one point and having to go back the coming weekend and play again before the home crowd is really no different than working really hard to make a sale and losing it or spending hours developing a wonderful marketing presentation and losing the client you were trying to win. They are both losses involving adversity or unfavorable and unpleasant experiences.

A player who has been traded during his career to more than just a few teams told me that the experience allowed him to be able to integrate into any team. It was, he said, no different than stepping into a new job in a new office and learning to work with new co-workers. Additionally, with new coaches and new teams came with a new "system" that he had to learn. While in the business world, his skill and ability to learn an entirely new playbook meant he feels comfortable learning a new company's business methods.

Another great transitional skill you have learned as a professional athlete is striving for a goal. As a team member, you wanted your team to win. Therefore, you have the skill of being competitive. You want yourself and your business team to achieve the goals you have set for yourself and the ones your business team has set for itself.

Most of all, as an athlete, you want to continually improve your skills and your game. "Better today than yesterday." You can transfer that skill, that mindset, into the business world as you transition from your old life to your new one.

CHAPTER 3

THE DREAM TEAM

Great advisors can be compared to "life coaches" because they can help you manage some of the complex financial decisions throughout your business life. Great BUSINESS advisors will help you reach your business goals as well.

The THREE most important advisors are:

- Legal – every successful business has great Legal advisors
- Financial – Every successful business has a great CPA
- Mentor – Every successful business person has a Mentor

Part of "working" with your team means understanding what they do, what recommendations they are making and more importantly WHY they are making those recommendations.

Be aware you may need more than one lawyer because you may need legal advice and representation for various things. For instance, if you want to transfer your business to the family, you would need an estate planning attorney. If you have bought a franchise or have started your own business, you may need a business attorney to help with possible business problems or help you set up a corporation. Maybe a legal issue with your taxes might arise in which your CPA could not help. Then you would need a tax attorney. Maybe you want to sue someone, or perhaps you're being sued. You would need a litigating attorney or a defense attorney for those situations. You can use different lawyers for different purposes, depending upon what your legal needs are.

For your financial bookkeeping and tax preparation, a Certified Public Accountant is your best resource.

Although regulations are a little different in each state, Certified Public Accountants must have over one-hundred and fifty hours of college-level accounting classes, must pass a six-part test (which can take 2 ½ days) as well as maintaining their licenses with forty hours of continuing education every year. CPAs are constantly improving their skills and being educated on changing tax laws. For small businesses who don't have huge staff, the CPA acts as your CFO (Chief Financial Officer) integrated into your long term and more advanced financial affairs as well as Tax Planning.

When you start picking your team, make sure you pick a team that you think will work together and be able to act independently from one another. Make sure that if you want to terminate one of the three, that it won't affect your relationship with the other two.

How to Best Work with Your Team?

For your Business the right attorney will guide you in creating your entity legally and ensuring that your documents, corporate minutes are in order. This is KEY to maintaining the corporate structure AND the liability protection that it affords.

Also, your attorney will protect you and your company from threats both internal and external through a strong operating agreement, shareholder agreement or partnership agreement as we discussed earlier. Your attorney will draft employment agreements, non-solicitation, non-disclosure agreements to protect your business assets from internal theft from employees etc. If you can think it will happen, it might happen and your attorney is there to make sure you are legally protected

Next is your CPA, or Certified Public Accountant. Your small business must have the right CPA who will be indispensable for tax planning and tax return preparation. This is critical to long term business success. CPAs prepare business plans, help you execute those plans, work with banks to get you funding, work with your attorney's to draft business documents and help with the day to day financial reporting as well as forecasting, budgeting and planning.

CPAs also have clients in many different industries and understand the complex tax situations for your business as well as having experience consulting with other clients in your industry. Having a CPA Certification is a key qualification for proper tax planning advice.

Strong supportive professionals are key to success for any business. Without the help of strong legal and financial professionals, a business can risk being open to lawsuits, theft, embezzlement fraud, IRS Tax liens and possible jail time for errors of judgment.

Teamwork is vital. You know full well the absolute necessity of teamwork on a playing field, a basketball court, or crammed in a bobsled. Just as selecting a coaching team, it is absolutely critical that you carefully choose the business team. Periodic team meetings in which all professionals and you gather to discuss the business "game plan" are excellent in keeping everyone involved on the same page, running the same direction on the same track, and planning the same game.

It takes a well-oiled machine, a closely working team to create a successful Game Plan. Your continued success towards your goals will depend upon skillful, superior, and trustworthy teamwork.

Success. According to the dictionary, "success" means several things. It is an "achievement of intention," "something that turns out well," or an "attainment of fame, wealth, or power." Normally, success is wonderful when an intention is achieved or something turns out for the good. Attainment of fame, wealth, or power is a positive accomplishment as well. You're on the field, success breeds confidence in realizing intended athletic goals. It also can create a false confidence that success ON the field will spill over to success OFF the field. Highly successful professional athletes are vulnerable to pitfalls off the fields without the proper level of advice and a strong support team.

You should be aware of these similar feelings of invincibility. The ability and confidence for a boxer to step into the ring can be an asset or a detriment outside of the ring. But as we discussed previously, while you're ON the field accomplishments take a team of trainers, coaches and team- mates, your OFF the field success also requires a strong team of professionals.

YOU will always triumph with such a team supporting your goals and objectives as they align with a healthy, productive business and life plan.

Confidence. Confidence exhibits deep strength, poise, and sureness. Confidence is modest. Confidence drives success. A person can be assuredly confident in their athletic accomplishments and an ego driven by assured self-confidence is one which delivers top achievements in sports performance, performing arts, or any profession. A highly successful professional athlete is one who has bedrock self-confidence in their abilities to positively perform functions of their particular sport and attain its highest objectives. You have the confidence necessary to perform at the highest level of your sport. But it is critical that you realize and truly understand that your capabilities ON the field may not translate into the same abilities and success OFF the field.

The important point to remember is that having experienced coaches greatly aids in navigating the changing landscape of business life. Some challenges are fundamental business issues, and others are a complex matter of financial and legal decisions. I hope that you recognize the value of such guides, mentors, or experienced advisers and counselors.

Finally, finding a business Mentor.

In addition to the professional advisors, it is important that you find a Mentor. What is a Mentor? Where does one find a mentor? Who is a mentor? The Dictionary defines a mentor as an experienced and trusted adviser. The knowledge, advice, and resources of a mentor depends on how you develop and build your relationship with your mentor. Your mentoring relationship is personal and unique to you. A mentor may share information with you about his or her own career path, as well as provide guidance, motivation, and emotional support.

How to find a Mentor?

You may have already found your mentor or it may be someone you have not met yet. Networking is valuable in finding and building a relationship with a potential mentor. I have discussed networking previously and you may have to reach back to your "rolodex" of names and contacts to find that mentor

For a business mentor it may not be someone in the "business" but just someone who has your best interest at heart, is able to listen to your attorney and your CPA and give you the good advice you need to hear. It may be someone who is skilled in the industry you are operating and can guide you through, with experience, the world of industry. See Appendix III for more information on mentoring.

CHAPTER 4

CHOOSING YOUR BUSINESS

When you start this process it's important to evaluate which business opportunities are already available to you. You may have a friend, family or former teammate already in the type of business you want to explore. Perhaps, you may want to go back to school and study Law or Medicine to become an attorney, a doctor, physical therapist, coach, etc., the choices are endless.

Are you an outgoing person who loves to talk? Maybe you want to explore a position in Sales.

Perhaps you want to open and operate a local business. You may decide to open up a physical store, sometimes referred to a "brick and mortar". In other words, you have an office front, whether it be retail, whether it be the service industry but you have an actual physical business and you have an office. You have staff and you have people who go there and you have inventory; all of the things that go on with actually owning a business that sits inside of a physical building. This can be an original concept of your own, you can purchase an existing business or buy a franchise, which we will discuss later in the book.

In recent years many people have started online businesses or a *virtual* business. Many businesses don't actually need to have a physical building and you can operate the business from the comfort of your own home. Today, you can operate a business through as little as your own phone or laptop from the beach!

Going back to the decision of what you want to do, there are other factors such as lifestyle, kids, family, travel etc. It is important that no matter what business you choose it must make sense for you and your family.

When it comes to deciding what type of business and industry in which you want to get involved after your athletic career, it's important to also think about the level of education that may be required. Pursuing further education is not only time-consuming but it can be costly as well. Education may only be part of the process as you may be required to get additional certification, even to be a football coach, a basketball coach or maybe a fitness coach.

In some cases certifications can be required or just add to your credibility. In considering what you want to do, you also have to ask yourself, "Is this something that I'm willing to put forth the effort to become educated"? Having an education or certification helps further your career. It gives people comfort that you know what you are doing in addition to a level of comfort that you are willing to make the sacrifice of time and effort to get that additional education.

When deciding on the type of business or industry you should consider the essential aspects of the financial side of things.

Understanding the financial side of any business is critical to its success and must be thought through carefully before jumping into anything. While you may not understand *all* of the financial sides of a business, there are plenty of people who are experts. Those are the people you want to have in your advisory team.

Financially, when starting a business, it is important to understand the upfront or "start-up" costs. Questions such as "Do I have to go buy a bunch of trucks and equipment?" Or "is this something I can just start with a computer?"

Franchises are discussed later in the book, but are, in some cases, a great way for you to start a business because part of what you are buying is a "playbook" on how to run the business. Fortunately, prior to purchasing a franchise, the information about the company is included in what is known as a Franchise Disclosure Document (FDD). In some cases, they include only a few pages about the finances. The remaining 300 pages include notes about what you can and can't do as well as some of the history. This is a critical reason for having your advisory team involved in your decision.

Many of questions will need to be addressed with your advisory team including,

What are the numbers saying?

What is my risk and reward?

Am I going to have to invest a lot of money?

Risk starts with the startup costs. If there is little or no cost to start up, then you have less financial risk. It's only your time. The most important step in starting a business is to build a business plan in order to build your understanding of how to operate your potential new business.

CHAPTER 5

STARTUP

A new business requires careful planning and dedication in order to ensure success. It is an exciting and challenging process. By following the steps outlined above, entrepreneurs can increase their chances of success and create a thriving business.This chapter will provide an overview of the steps involved in starting a new business.

The first step in starting a new business is to choose a business structure. The most common business structures are sole proprietorships, partnerships, limited liability companies (LLCs), and corporations. Each type of business structure has its own advantages and disadvantages, so it is important to consider all of the options before deciding. (I will devote a chapter later to "entity choice")

The second step is to create a business plan. A business plan is a written document that outlines the goals and objectives of the business. It also includes information about the market, the customers, the competition, and the financial projections. A business plan is essential for obtaining financing and for convincing potential investors to invest in the business. (The following chapter goes into detail on the Business Plan)

The third step is to obtain the necessary licenses and permits. Depending on the type of business, there may be different licenses and permits required. It is important to research the applicable laws and regulations in order to ensure that all of the necessary licenses and permits are obtained.

The fourth step is to create a marketing plan. A marketing plan is a written document that outlines the strategies and tactics that will be used to promote the business. It includes information about target markets, advertising, promotions, pricing, and customer service.

The fifth step is to obtain financing. Financing is necessary in order to purchase equipment, supplies, and other materials needed to start the business. It is important to research different financing options and to compare interest rates and terms before deciding.

Finally, the sixth step is to launch the business. This involves opening the business and marketing the products or services to potential customers. It is important to ensure that the business is properly staffed and that the necessary systems and processes are in place before launching.

Starting a new business is an exciting and challenging process. It requires careful planning and dedication in order to ensure success. By following the steps outlined above, entrepreneurs can increase their chances of success and create a thriving business.

Once you have considered which industry suits you and what's best for your personal life, you may be wondering... *what absolutely must be in place for the business plan to be successful? What is an operating agreement? What are the potential things that could happen and how to protect yourself?*

What is an Operating Agreement? When we talk about starting a business, one of the most important things from a legal standpoint is to have the correct documentation that establishes the rules of your company. In some cases, you will have a business partner or an investor. In which case proper legal agreements must be prepared upfront.

Most people don't sign prenuptial agreements because they are getting *married*. They sign a prenuptial agreement in case they get *divorced*. Similarly, operating agreements with partnerships and S corporations and even bylaws of a corporation are all necessary for the *end* game. I have seen many clients have horrible legal battles because they did not invest in the company up front to document the rules and ended up in a fight when things went wrong.

The point is to make sure that you do not go into a new business with just a handshake and a buddy. You really do need the right operating agreements and the right documents to make sure that both parties understand the rules and the roles. Who gets to do what and who has authority over certain decisions. Consider these questions: *Who gets to make the final decision? What if we can't decide? What happens if somebody dies? What happens if somebody becomes disabled? What happens if somebody quits? Who can sell the business?* You have to consider the best and worst-case scenarios. The bottom line is you don't walk into a stadium or out onto the court without a game plan. So, don't walk into a business without a proper business plan.

Entity Choice

If you tell people you are starting a business, you will hear a variety of things; *you should be an S corporation, you should be an LLC, a corporation, a partnership, etc. The correct answer is* "it depends."

The answers to all these choices can depend on factors such as *"Am I going to bring in partners?* Is this going to be a family business where you're going to want to bring in your children, maybe a brother or sister, or an aunt or uncle? This comes back to choice of entity. *How is it going to be taxed and all of the other decisions that go into what type of entity should you choose?*

The best type of entity for you may not be the best for someone else. Some types of entities are created for liability protection and some are to save taxes. Some are to protect the assets inside the company. Some are created to allow you to give shares of stock to valued employees.

One of the next decisions is to choose a name for your ocmpany. It can be something as simple as International Business Machines (IBM) for example. It's straightforward, easy to remember and everybody will recognize it. Additionally, your name becomes your brand. If you come up with a name it is important to register that name with your state. You don't want to use a company name, build up a brand only to find out that there is already a business using the same or similar name. You may end up in a legal battle to keep your name which could destroy your brand value and all your hard work.

Per the Small Business Administration (www.sba.gov) there are four different ways to register your business name

Entity Name

An entity name can protect the name of your business at a state level. Depending on your business structure and location, the state may require you to register a legal entity name.

Your entity name is how the state identifies your business. Each state may have different rules about what your entity name can be and usage of company suffixes. Most states don't allow you to register a name that's already been registered by someone else, and some states require your entity name to reflect the kind of business it represents.

In most cases, your entity name registration protects your business and prevents anyone else in the state from operating under the same entity name. However, there are exceptions pertaining to state and business structure.

Trademark

A trademark can protect the name of your business, goods, and services at a national level. Trademarks prevent others in the same (or similar) industry in the United States from using your trademarked names.

For example, if you were an electronics company and wanted to call your business Springfield Electronic Accessories and one of your products is the Screen Cover 5000. By trademarking those names it would prevent other electronics businesses or similar products from using those same names.

Businesses in every state are subject to trademark infringement lawsuits, which can prove costly. That's why you should check your prospective business, product and service names against the official trademark database maintained by the United States Patent and Trademark Office.

Doing business as (DBA) name

You might need to register your DBA — also known as a trade name, fictitious name, or assumed name — with the state, county, or city in which your business is located. Registering your DBA name doesn't provide legal protection by itself, but most states require you to register your DBA if you use one. Some business structures require you to use a DBA.

Even if you're not required to register a DBA, you might want to anyway. A DBA lets you conduct business under a different identity from your own personal name or your formal business entity name. As an added bonus, getting a DBA and federal tax ID number (EIN) allows you to open a business bank account.

Multiple businesses can go by the same DBA in one state, so you are less restricted in what you can choose. There is also more leeway in the clarity of business function. For example, a small business owner could use Springfield Electronic Accessories for their entity name but use Tec Buddy for their DBA. Just remember that trademark infringement laws will still apply.

Determine your DBA requirements based on your specific location. Requirements vary by business structure as well as by state, county, and municipality, so check with local government offices and websites.

Domain name

If you want an online presence for your business, start by registering a domain name — also known as your website address, or URL.

Once you register your domain name, no one else can use it for as long as you continue to own it. It's a good way to protect your brand presence online.

If someone else has already registered the domain you wanted to use, that is okay. Your domain name does not actually need to be the same as your legal business name, trademark, or DBA. For example, Springfield Electronic Accessories could register the domain name techbuddyspringfield.com.

A domain name is registered through a registrar service. Consult a directory of accredited registrars to determine which ones are safe to use, and then pick one that offers you the best combination of price and customer service. You'll need to renew your domain registration on a regular basis.

In fact, some athletes – such as Michael Jordan, Donovan McNabb, Tiger Woods and Natalie Gulbis – have filed for trademark protection of their names. Magic Johnson has a trademark on Earvin "Magic" Johnson. There are many athletes and "famous" people who have secured their name to make sure that their brand has value as being unique.

THE OPERATING AGREEMENT aka "THE RULE BOOK"

Depending on they choice of entity, this can also be called a Shareholders Agreement if you are operating as a corporation or an Operating Agreement if you are an LLC or a Partnership agreement if you are operating as a Partnership.

Regardless of what it is called, THIS is the rule book for your company.

The SBA website states that an operating agreement is a key document used by companies because it outlines the business' financial and functional decisions including rules, regulations and provision. The purpose of the document is to govern the internal operations of the business in a way that suits the specific needs of the business owners. Once the document is signed by the members of the limited liability company, it acts as an official contract binding them to its terms.

Why do you need an operating agreement?

1. To protect the business' limited liability status: Operating agreements give members protection from personal liability of the company. Without this specific formality, your company can closely resemble a sole proprietorship or partnership, jeopardizing your personal liability.

2. To clarify verbal agreements: Even if members have orally agreed to certain terms, misunderstanding or miscommunication can take place. It is always best to have the operational conditions and other business arrangements handled in writing so they can be referred to in the event of any conflict.

3. To protect your agreement in the eyes of your state: State default rules govern companies without an official operating agreement. This means that each state outlines default rules that apply to businesses that do not sign operating agreements. Because the state default rules are so general, it is not advisable to rely on a governing body state to manage your agreement.

Tip: Consult with an attorney and accountant to assist with the financial and legal matters of your agreement.

What does an operating agreement entail?

Operating agreements are contract documents that are generally between five and twenty pages long.

What is included in an operating agreement?

The functionality of internal affairs is outlined in the operating agreement including but not limited to:

- Percentage of members' ownership
- Voting rights and responsibilities

- Powers and duties of members and managers
- Distribution of profits and losses
- Holding meetings
- Buyout and buy-sell rules (procedures for transferring interest or in the event of a death)

Are LLCs required to form an operating agreement?

The requirement of an operating agreement depends on the state in which it was formed. Many states do not require operating agreements. This information can generally be found on your Secretary of State website.

WARNING: Although some states do not require an operating agreement it is unwise to operate without an operating agreement. Regardless of your state's law, think twice before opting out of this provision.

Where should operating agreements be kept?

Operating agreements should be kept with the core records of your business. They are not required to be filed, nor will they be accepted by your state.

Some of the other pieces you'll find in an operating agreement include tax decisions, what types of meetings you'll have, what *is* actually defined as a meeting, and who gets to make certain decisions? Who is the managing member? What do we do? Is this operating agreement based upon the laws upon the state you are in? And if there is a dispute, do we file that dispute in New York, in California, in Arizona?

Again, all of these questions are reasons why it is important to make sure that you have got a really good attorney. Someone who you can trust is going to go through that operating agreement with a fine-tooth comb. While it can be hard to imagine *every* possible scenario, a good operating agreement will cover *most* of those scenarios.

CAUTION: Make sure the operatizing agreement is not too short or too long. In a recent case, one client had a 75 page operating agreement that was so complicated when the partners wanted to split up no one could figure out how to split up the assets of the company and how to resolve the differences. If you make the rules make sure you understand them. If you are the main owner, make sure they protect YOU and YOUR assets.

CHAPTER 6

BUSINESS PLAN

A business plan is the GAME PLAN for any business, whether it is a start-up or an established business. A business plan can help a business owner identify the goals and objectives of the business, as well as how to reach those goals and objectives. It also provides a roadmap for the business and helps to keep it on track. This book will discuss the importance of a business plan and provide details on a business plan for a start-up business.

The importance of a Business Plan is no different than a well crafted GAME PLAN.

A business plan is an essential document for any business as it outlines the objectives of the business, the strategies for achieving those objectives, and the resources that will be needed to achieve them. A business plan also helps to identify potential risks and opportunities as well as how to manage them. Furthermore, a business plan can be used to attract investors, lenders, and other stakeholders.

The initial step building a business plan for a start-up business is to identify the goals and objectives of the business, as well as a roadmap to reach them. It also helps to identify potential risks and opportunities and how you will manage them.

Parts of a Business Plan

This example of a business plan is for a start-up business. The business is a retail store that specializes in selling high-end clothing and accessories.

Objectives

The objectives of the business are to:

1. Generate sales of $1 million in the first year of operation.
2. Achieve profitability in the second year of operation.
3. Increase sales by 10% each year.
4. Establish a strong customer base and positive reputation in the community.
5. Develop an online presence to increase sales.

Strategies

The strategies for achieving the objectives of the business are to:

1. Offer a wide selection of high-end clothing and accessories.
2. Develop a loyalty program to encourage repeat customers.
3. Utilize social media and other digital marketing tools to increase brand awareness and sales.
4. Establish relationships with local designers and fashion bloggers to increase brand awareness.
5. Develop an online store to increase sales.

Resources

The resources needed to achieve the objectives of the business are:

1. A retail space in a high-traffic area.

2. A website and online store.

3. A point-of-sale system.

4. A marketing budget for advertising and promotional activities.

5. A staff of sales associates.

Similar to a game situation, you will constantly analyze all possible outcomes to be able to react to different possible scenarios. Additionally, a well-done business plan can also be used to keep track of your business with targets and performance analysis. A business plan is a great way to hold yourself accountable as you move into your new career.

The parts of the business plan include 5 major aspects of the business:

1. Executive Summary

2. Organization and Management

3. Sales and Marketing

4. Finances

5. SWOT

To start a business plan, start with an Executive Summary, which tells your reader a little about you and your ideas (www.sba.gov). Sometimes I will tailor this specific to the person who may be reading the plan. If we are presenting to a bank it may be slightly different than if we are looking for private investors.

PART 1: Executive summary

Briefly tell your reader what your company is and why it will be successful. Include your mission statement, your product or service, and basic information about your company's leadership team, employees, and location. You should also include financial information and high-level growth plans if you plan to ask for financing.

Company description

Use your company description to provide detailed information about your company. Go into detail about the problems your business solves. Be specific, and list out the consumers, organization, or businesses your company plans to serve.

Explain the competitive advantages that will make your business a success. Are there experts on your team? Have you found the perfect location for your store? Your company description is the place to boast about your strengths.

Market analysis

You'll need a good understanding of your industry outlook and target market. Competitive research will show you what other businesses are doing and identify their strengths. In your market research, look for trends and themes. What do successful competitors do? Why does it work? Can you do it better?

PART 2: Organization and Management

Tell your reader how your company will be structured and who will run it. Describe the legal structure of your business. State whether you have or intend to incorporate your business as a C or an S corporation, form a general or limited partnership, or if you're a sole proprietor or limited liability company (LLC). (More on Structure later in the book)

Use an organizational chart to lay out who's in charge of what in your company. Show how each person's unique experience will contribute to the success of your venture. Consider including resumes and "curriculum vitae" of key members of your team. In other words, tell them why this company WILL be successful. Also, don't BS, readers can smell that a mile away, be honest clear and speak with positive attitude but back it up with hard numbers.

PART 3: Sales and Marketing

Time to tell the reader how you are going to Execute the PLAN

Describe what you sell or what service you offer. Explain how it benefits your customers and what the product life cycle looks like. Share your plans for intellectual property, like copyright or patent filings. If you're doing research and development for your service or product, explain it in detail.

Marketing and sales sections talk about HOW you are going to "get it done"

There's no single way to approach a marketing strategy. Your strategy should evolve and change to fit your unique needs.

Your goal in this section is to describe how you'll attract and retain customers. You'll also describe how a sale will actually happen. You'll refer to this section later when you make financial projections, so make sure to thoroughly describe your complete marketing and sales strategies.

Part 4: MONEY

If you're asking for funding, this is where you'll outline your funding requirements. Your goal is to clearly explain how much funding you'll need over the next five years and what you'll use it for.

Specify whether you want debt or equity, the terms you'd like applied, and the length of time your request will cover. Give a detailed description of how you'll use your funds. Specify if you need funds to buy equipment or materials, pay salaries, or cover specific bills until revenue increases. Always include a description of your future strategic financial plans, like paying off debt or selling your business.

Financial projections

Supplement your funding request with financial projections. Your goal is to convince the reader that your business is stable and will be a financial success.

If your business is already established, include income statements, balance sheets, and cash flow statements for the last three to five years. If you have collateral you need use to secure a loan, make sure to list it in your plan.

Provide a prospective financial outlook for the next five years. Include forecasted income statements, balance sheets, cash flow statements, and capital expenditure budgets. For the first year, be even more specific and use quarterly — or even monthly — projections. Make sure to clearly explain your projections, and match them to your funding requests.

This is a great place to use graphs and charts to tell the financial story of your business.

PART 5: The SWOT analysis

I know it sounds funny, but it's key that you let your reader know this is not a Pie in the Sky dream and that you have actually thought about the problems that may occur and possible roadblocks to your success. If you do not analyze those, how will you know how to beat your competitors. How you plan to break through to achieve your success?

SWOT analysis stands for Strengths, Weaknesses, Opportunities, and Threats. It forces you to analyze the business before you start.

Many people don't really realize what it takes to start a business but also are not prepared or equipped for success. You have to ready yourself for not just starting a business but operating that business as well– through all of the highs and lows.

The most important thing to understand is that starting a business is no different than if you are preparing for the start of the season or preparing for a game. You need to have your game plan set, have good coaches and advisors to encourage you and be available for any questions you have. What are all of the different ways to approach a certain play or situation? Do you have people in your corner to help in a pinch? Do you have a backup plan in case the game changes unexpectedly? Ask yourself, what are my alarms? What are the things I need to be aware of? And when I see them, what do I need to do to react?

There are may professionals that can assist with preparation of a business plan. As a CPA I have prepare many plans and projections for clients. Your plan may need to be more technical and you may need a specialist that prepares business plans for complex industries. Note that the cost of a business plan can run $5,000 to $25,000.

CHAPTER 7

ENTITY CHOICE

The first question I get asked when we get a new client is "do I need an LLC?" The answer is "maybe". First you must understand what an LLC is and what you can use it for. An LLC can give you an opportunity to save some taxes, but it can also help Create, Expand and Protect your BRAND.

Liability protection. An LLC is a separate legal entity that shields your personal assets from lawsuits or debts related to your business activities. For example, if someone sues you for breach of contract or defamation, they can only go after the assets of the LLC, not your personal bank accounts or property.

Tax flexibility. An LLC can choose how it wants to be taxed by the IRS. You can elect to be taxed as a sole proprietorship, a partnership, or a corporation. Depending on your income level and expenses, you may be able to save money on taxes by choosing the best option for your situation.

LLC WARNING: DO NOT DO THIS YOURSELF,
HIRE A PROFESSIONAL

Choose a name for your LLC. The name should be unique, catchy, and related to your brand identity. You also need to make sure that the name is not already taken by another business in your state. You can check the availability of names on the website of the state agency that handles business filings (usually the Secretary of State)

Designate a registered agent. A registered agent is a person or company that agrees to receive legal documents on behalf of your LLC. The registered agent must have a physical address in the state where you form your LLC. You can choose anyone who meets these requirements, including your- self, a friend, a family member, or a professional service company.

File articles of organization. Articles of organization are the official documents that create your LLC with the state. They usually include information such as the name and address of the LLC, the name and address of the registered agent, the purpose and duration of the LLC, and the names of the members (owners) of the LLC. You can file these documents online or by mail with the state agency that handles business filings.

Create an operating agreement. An operating agreement is a document that outlines how your LLC will be run and how decisions will be made. It can cover topics such as how profits and losses will be distributed, how taxes will be paid, how new members will be admitted or existing members will exit, and how disputes will be resolved. Although an operating agreement is not required by most states, it is highly recommended to have one to avoid potential conflicts and confusion among members.

Get an employer identification number (EIN). An EIN is a unique number assigned by the IRS to identify your LLC for tax purposes. You need an EIN to open a bank account for your LLC, file tax returns, hire employees, and apply for licenses and permits. You can apply for an EIN online for free on the IRS website.

CHAPTER 8

RUNNING THE BUSINESS

Now the doors are open, the website is live, and you are in business. *Now what?*

Well, now it's game time and as we all know during games, things happen. Players get hurt. The weather changes. People make mistakes. It is important that you understand when you own your own company, the business is going to go through different phases. You need to have the realization that you are going to have good times and bad times. Hopefully you are going to have really GREAT times.

So how do you plan for the Ups and Downs of a business?

Because of COVID-19, 2020 was a very difficult year for many of my clients and a great year for others. Some businesses did horrible and went out of business while others were able to pivot and create opportunities to survive and thrive.

The ones that did well were able to because they had a good plan. For instance, one of my restaurant clients had to completely pivot from being a brick and mortar restaurant to being an online delivery food service– and they doubled their revenue.

Those times are also when friends, family, advisors, and mentors will come into play. People who know how to pivot when a situation arises so that you can maintain your business. These are key people to have in your corner and on your team during times like these!

How much should be done in terms of preplanning potential hiccups and problems? And then what can be done during those hiccups and problems?

Planning for problems, changes, and contingencies is often difficult. For example, if your business is in a hurricane zone, there needs to be a plan. If you have a business that relies heavily on a specific industry, then there has to be a plan. *What if something happens in that industry?* Sometimes you can plan by looking at what has happened in the past and what might repeat. Other times you just are not able to plan for every possible problem.

One typical problem that can occur is the loss of a key employee. Your office manager may be someone you rely on for your operations. Your key salesperson may be the core to your business growth. When that employee quits or his or her spouse gets a job somewhere else and he or she has to move, you have to be prepared as the business owner.

Cross training other staff to do some of that work can help, but it's actually more important that you, as the business owner, should know how to do everybody's jobs. That way, if you lose someone in your business or if they are out sick, or there was any other type of problem, you could fill in pretty much any piece of the job. While you may not necessarily *want* to, either you or someone in your business is going to be able to jump in and fill in. So cross-training is also very, very important.

You also need to have a contingency plan in place for a business loss. Make sure you have the right insurance because you never know if and when there may be a problem. Consider any potential damage – from fires to hurricanes – and think about whether or not you have the right insurance that's going to help you get through that period of time while you're rebuilding your business.

Some of these issues that you need to be aware of are *economic* in nature. Most of these are out of your control. Inflation, resulting in price increases in your supplies or product used to manufacture your product. In other words, if your business uses plastic, which is a petroleum-based product, you are dependent upon the price of oil. If the cost of oil rises significantly, you need to be prepared.

Weather can also create economic issues. If there is a hurricane, a snowstorm or anything that would affect your ability to get supplies or your own product to the store you need to be prepared.

The key here is to create a business that is *nimble*. Not just one that can make a permanent change as the economy changes, but a business that is also able to "weather the storm." Some businesses have an advantage of being all cloud-based so when COVID hit and everybody had to work from home, it was no different than if they were working in the office. If you were all set up on a server and you had no way for your staff to remotely and securely log in, then you were stuck. The IRS, as an example, took *six months* to figure out how to be able to let people work from home in the middle of COVID. To repeat, sometimes there is a permanent change in you situation and sometimes it's temporary. Thus the importance of having the ability to be nimble.

REGULATIONS become important when you own a business. What are some things to consider related to staff, government regulations, etc.?

While government regulations can be one of the most common difficulties to deal with in a business, finding staff, let alone *qualified* staff, becomes another. Staff, these days, will leave for a 50-cent raise, believe it or not. Some employees will just not show up to work because they don't *feel* like it. If you are not prepared for these situations, it may do some damage to your business and your reputation of always being on time or always being responsive.

Government regulations deal with your business in many ways.

1 – Licensing

2 – Human Resources (employee rights)

3 – Taxes and Reporting

For instance, as a CPA I am guided by the IRS regulations. If there are pronouncements or regulations that the IRS changes, I am required to be knowledgeable about those law changes.

If you own a restaurant, you need to be aware of health codes. If you are a manufacturing business, you need to be aware of workers compensation rules, safety rules also known as OSHA, Occupational Safety and Health Administration rules. These are just two of the many *government regulations that can affect your business.*

So, the question you need to ask yourself is, "Are you ready for those changes?" Does your business plan have the capability to be able to move with changes in the industry? While nobody can predict what's going to happen, you do have to be aware of the most current rules within your industry.

Being able to be nimble, quick, and not averse to change is going to keep you successful.

Tips on Growing your Business
How to Network and Brand your business

Networking, it's not what you know…In her book Fit for Business, Taylor Pak states that when she was recruited for college soccer, "you have limited time to show a coach who you are and what potential you have." "Trying to master your elevator speech at the age of 16 is difficult." However, she realized that the experience helped and guided her in realizing that she had already had many "job interviews."

"It's fair to say that the recruiting process is equitable to the … [business sales] process, which means that … athletes already have a great deal of practice."

As an athlete, you already have the tools and experience of "selling yourself". Now you just have to sell "your business" Taylor states that "it's OK to feel uncertainty and discomfort … about the next chapter of your life because you have the OPPORTUNITY to make something of yourself."

There's an old saying in business that "it's not what you know but who you know," which holds very true in today's business environment.

Networking can make a huge difference a business succeeding or failing

Now what do I do?

Harvey MacKay, a well-known syndicated columnist, author and business networking guru, talks about knowing your contact and how critical that knowledge is to be able to grow and maintain a business. It's the same way for a student- athlete and as professional athlete with one major benefit. As a former athlete, you may have the ability to get your "foot in the door" where others cannot.

You have an opportunity to interact with alumni and boosters, all of whom may be successful business people in the community.

When attending charity events, it is important that you "kick butt and take names." More importantly, keep the information of whom you met. You may want to have somebody help you follow up after meetings through email, calling or setting up a lunch. Meeting those contacts can be beneficial, especially if they can help you with a project running your business. Take advantage of the opportunities presented to you.

Wayne Kimmel, in his book "Six Degrees of Wayne Kimmel," the networking guru and venture capitalist at Seventy-Six Capital has "the Gospel" for networking.

How do you meet the people that will become your most trusted and influential relationships? You have to go out and find them. You never know who (sic) they're going to be, so you have to cast as wide a net as possible."

There are two things to remember in networking. First, the "never say no" attitude. Kareem Abdul Jabar's advice is to get out there and "engage?" While you don't want to overdo your schedule, you never know what new opportunities will come from attending an event. The other is from BNI Networking, "Givers Gain." This means that you should find out how you can help them, and in return they will want to help you. Many athletes do not realize that you have the power to meet anyone. If LeBron James wanted to meet the president of any fortune 100 company, Microsoft, Uber, Amazon it would only take one phone call. While you may not be LeBron, you still have a great opportunity to meet people in your community.

Create your contact list, what used to be known as a Rolodex. While many of you are being taught how to use LinkedIn, note that this platform, unlike Instagram, is more professional.

Community and business leaders are most of the attendees at these events and it's a great opportunity for you to meet people who might be able to help you transition from your "sporting world" to the "regular world" when that time comes. I urge you to get comfortable and be open to every opportunity you have and build your network of meaningful contacts.

Your meaningful contacts are people you know something about. They are not just a connection you made by clicking "Accept." You want to know about their jobs, their hobbies, their birthdays or family members; you may have some common business acquaintances. The longer you are in business, the more you network, the more your contacts may become your friends as well.

Do not be surprised, but they will be far more interested in YOUR stories of being an athlete. Build your networking file. Follow up with people you've met. Go to events. Develop real friendships with people outside of your athletic world. Grow your support system. As a professional athlete, you have a wonderful opportunity to network.

More gospel from Wayne: "there will be nights when you would rather hangout with your family and friends instead of going to a networking, political or charity event. GO ANYWAY. You never know who you will meet. This is a long game. Building relationships is like a marathon, not a sprint."

Building Brand Value
Your business BRAND

First, what is branding? Simply put, in the retail world, a brand is something that identifies a product or an idea in people's minds. For example, "Kleenex" conjures up a small paper tissue in people's minds whether or not that tissue is a Kleenex brand tissue, Puff, or Angel Soft. If you sneezed, you probably would say to me, "Hand me a Kleenex, please." I doubt if you would ask me to hand you a facial tissue. Other common, successful retail brands include Saran Wrap and Band Aids and hundreds of other household names.

Want to grow your business? Then NETWORK NETWORK NETWORK! With every hand you shake and with every post you post, build your fine, strong, outstanding brand!

Networking Reminders

- Get out there
- Follow Up
- Don't be shy
- Get a Wingman

CHAPTER 9

BUSINESS GROWTH

Growth can be good or bad. We've talked a little bit about pivoting and being able to manage a business when things change. So, now let's talk about what happens if things get really good. *Are you ready for that?*

There have been times when things got really good, really fast, and the business was not prepared. All of a sudden, you are chasing your tail, trying to catch up. This happens when you do not have the right systems in place to manage 500 new customers overnight. When we talk about business planning it is critical to look at both the good and the bad.

What I tell my clients when they start any business is "what is your exit strategy."

What is your vision for today? Tomorrow? But more importantly where do you want to be 5-10 years in the future.

When things go well, you need to have a plan for the growth? Do you reinvest it in the business? Is now a good time to sell? Do you want to give something extra to your employees? Business growth is great, but you have to be prepared for all of the possible scenarios.

Cash Needs for Growth

What happens if you need money for growth? Should you put your own money into the business or should you borrow money and create debt.

What to do when it comes to debt? What is good? What is bad? Should you operate a business with no debt, or should you operate a business with debt?

Every consultant has a different view on borrowing money. Debt allows you to expand a business without needing the cash right now. However, debt must be repaid. When you borrow money to expand or grow, you still need a plan on how to repay that debt.

Alternatively, you could wait to accumulate the cash and *then* buy the new machine, or whatever it is that would benefit your business. Or you could borrow the money and start benefiting *now*.

Help Wanted

What are some recommendations on partners, talent, and giving ownership to other people?

What happens when you need more help and more staff? How do you determine who you need to help your business growth continue? Do I bring in an employee or add a partner?

Staffing

In MY business we have three types of staff. Minders, Finders and Grinders and you need all three. The Finder is someone who is going to go out and find business, they are going to keep a steady flow of new clients. This is your sales leader. A Minder is the person that is going to take care of the clients on an ongoing basis. This person is key to making sure that the new business stays with your company. Finally, the Grinder is your hard worker. The grinder is critical to making sure that the work gets done and gets done correctly. Each of these three key employees require different skills and different personalities.

If a partner is your decision, you have to figure out if it is the *right* partner? Is that partner going to help you? Is that partner going to make the business better? Is that partner going to bring other resources and skills to the table?

When is the *right time* to bring in a partner? There is no right answer. The answer is probably right when you need it. Of course, some people need a partner right at the outset because they can't do it alone.

All partners have certain skills, just like in any team. There may be an offense, defense and special teams. Some people are really good at sales. Some people are really good at numbers. Some people are really good at coming up with a vision.

CHAPTER 10

CUTTING LOSSES

When changes in your business or industry that are out of your control, even if you did your planning, it may be time to decide if you want to Sink or Swim.

In some cases, you have to finance the required changes necessary to survive. It may require personnel changes, location or an entire revamp of your business plan.

What do you need to do to improve things? Do you need to go to the bank and borrow some money? We talked a little bit about when it's a good time to use debt; if you are going to go and borrow money, you better have a really good reason and a really good plan because if you're not doing well, the bank will not loan money without a plan. The bank wants to make sure that you are going to use the money wisely. So, financing the required changes might be a good fix in the short term until you get things back on track. Alternatively, you might need to finance a new piece of equipment because the old one died or a newer technology is necessary to maintain the business.

Option two may be finding equity investors. Bringing in a partner who is going to invest in your company.

Option three may be to look at our customers or our competitors or Suppliers. Perhaps you team up. While you may have two struggling businesses individually, together it could be a bigger, better, thriving business.

Finally, it could be coming out of your own pocket or through friends and family.

How do you know when to close the doors? What are the options there?

Knowing when to completely shut the doors and stop your business is a very tough decision. Nobody really knows when that road will end and when that time comes, it's a very hard personal decision and you will have to go to your advisors and your mentors.

Remember that one of the most important things to realize going back to day one when you set up your business, is that you have to have an exit plan.

Note that it may not be a disaster plan but you always want to know how you will handle adversity.

If disaster occurs, you need to have a plan. Questions that you need to be able to answer include; Are you personally guaranteeing all those loans? Which means that if the business cannot repay a loan or an equipment lease, they are going to come after you for the money. Did you personally guarantee ten years of rent? Perhaps you have only been there for three years, which means you are obligated to pay seven years of rent or you have to negotiate yourself out of a lease.

Do you have liability protection in case that your customers are looking for an order and, for whatever reason, you now cannot meet that obligation? Do you have the money to issue a refund?

Planning for failure is not pleasant but is necessary.

What if you have partners or investors? Is your operating agreement and the structure of your company, the LLC, the s-corps, the C corporation setup to protect YOU? Have you done everything in your power to make sure that when things are bad, you are at least personally protected from losing everything?

Operating any business can be difficult. Operating a business successfully is even more difficult. The most important thing you can do is to make sure that you are set up ahead of time for when disaster strikes and that you are prepared. It's very similar to having auto insurance. You have auto insurance and you pay for it. You just hope you never have to use it.

CHAPTER 11

CHANGING WITH THE TIMES

No matter what business you are running, it is critical to be adaptable. Consider CPAs who have, traditionally, always dealt with paper. Now, there's a huge push for everything to be digital and paperless in an effort to work fully on an online platform. Now, because of COVID, we are now forced to be mobile and flexible using Zoom, Microsoft Teams and now in-person meetings suddenly became meetings on the computer.

It is important for any business to understand what the next stage of technology is going to be. What is your business going to face as time moves forward and technology continues to advance? Now, we are seeing AI (artificial intelligence) beginning to grow to a point that they may replace humans. It is critical to understand that some technology in the future may completely change your business model.

Bed Bath and Beyond as well as numerous retail stores are closing because they could not keep up with Amazon or Walmart through an online presence. Their customers changed how they buy and those companies that were not able to "pivot" failed or are failing.

Changes to the trucking industry are being discussed including autonomous electric trucks. Regardless of what industry you are in, it is important to understand the future technology that will either hurt or help your business. Remember that if you are not prepared and your competitors are ready, you may be left in the dust. Technology can also work in your favor to streamline processes, save money and deliver a better product more quickly to your customers.

How does blockchain technology affect finance and business?

By now most people know about Bitcoin. It is a type of digital currency in which a record of transactions is maintained and new units of currency are generated by the computational solution of mathematical problems, and which operates independently of a central bank. Bitcoin cryptocurrency is built on a platform known as blockchain technology. The blockchain technology is such that it builds trust between two parties that are involved in a transaction. While everybody looks at cryptocurrency as a possible way to transact commerce in the future, the backbone of Bitcoin, blockchain technology may end up being used in almost every single business transaction.

An example would be that the two biggest blockchain technology businesses that are implementing and consulting with blockchain technology are Visa and IBM. These large, well-known and established companies are trying to figure out how they can use blockchain technology to track inventory, supply chain management, knowing when products or raw materials are ordered to the point where artificial intelligence will know that as soon as something sold, it's already on the order list back to the supplier so that it can be replaced to be sold again.

Blockchain technology is starting to enter the healthcare industry so your medical records are going to be easily accessible anywhere in the world. Do you need to know everything about this new Technology? No, but it is something that you need to know exists. You don't have to understand *how* it works or even how to use it, just make sure that you have the experts on your side who understand how it may affect your business.

I wanted to discuss "technology in advertising. There are many different forms of advertising, and it is changing daily. Electronic billboards that follow you as you drive, customized ads on your phone based on what you watch and way too much about your personal habits; commercials on streaming services, Sporting events etc. We are being inundated with what is about to be customized advertising where you only see what you are interested in seeing.

Facebook has recently been hit hard by the fact that they are driven more by their advertising revenue than their possible social responsibility. Advertising online is *critical* right now for any business because that's where a lot of people are getting their customers. Now the most important thing is to understand that *you need to be where your customers are.*

Google advertising may not be where you need to be because your customers don't find you. For example, a CPA might not necessarily want the customers that are looking for a CPA just by Googling "CPA." You have to consider how to advertise and, if you have a website, how you're going to attract the *right* clients or customers. You may want to find very specific people; the artists, the entertainers, or sports figures who are looking for someone or something very specific.

How you use technology to advertise is also a matter of being smart with your dollars. You can spend a lot of money on Google, but if your clients don't go on Google, it's a waste of money. It's no different than if you were to put a billboard on a street where none of your customers drive. Understanding your customers and how you can reach them more effectively and efficiently.

There are a lot of companies out there who will tell you they will make you the number one search result on Google; and that is great, IF that's where your customers are looking.

What about utilizing social media?

Along the same theme of knowing where your customers are, social media can become a fantastic way to reach out to people who want to buy your products but may not know that your products are there. If you are in business as a consultant, you may want to use social media to post certain stories of why you're an expert in a certain field or react to certain stories that you see on the news of how your business helps those types of customers or those types of people. If you are a CPA, you will want to react to articles that involve finance, and specifically those that pertain to the same types of clients you service. If it is something about an athlete or an entertainer and taxes or finances or something that has to do with money, then you will want to react or respond if that is where your potential clients exist. It is a great opportunity for you to make yourself known as an expert in a specific field. You can go on social media and post something, and people will see it and it may resonate with them.

But you may not necessarily want to post about something that is unrelated to your business. Nobody necessarily wants to hear a CPA's opinion about catching fish or a CPA's opinion about a restaurant because that's not really their expertise. Knowing what social media outlets reach your clients is critical. Regardless if it is Instagram, Twitter(X), LinkedIn, Facebook, or any of the others, remember to find the expert. You do not have to do everything yourself, just make sure you have somebody who knows what they are doing and is able to effectively use those platforms to drive business for your company.

CHAPTER 12

EXIT STRATEGY

You always want to enter into any venture with an exit strategy in mind because you want to have a goal. That strategy may change over time and during the life of your business. You may start a business and have a child who may be very interested in taking over the family business. However, by the time they graduate college they are no longer interested. The opposite could be true as well. You may have a child who you do not anticipate going into the business and then over time they decide they would like to be a part of the family business.

Despite the numerous uncertainties that have impacted organizations in recent years—rising inflation, higher interest rates and the COVID-19 pandemic among them—the decision to sell or merge a family business remains usually specific to each company. It usually is a function of the family's circumstances, tends to be less cyclical in nature, and often has much more to do with the life experience of the owner and his or her family than anything else.

Most sale decisions among founder-owned companies tend to be closely tied to the personal situation of the founder(s). According to AARP, nearly half of all baby boomers (45%) consider themselves "entrepreneurs." With about 10,000 of them reaching retirement age each day, it's no surprise that many are motivated to consider a sale regardless of market conditions.

One recurring trend we have seen over the past several decades is that for many family-owned enterprises the next generation has shown little interest in taking over the business. As sons and daughters of founders choose to pursue their own career paths, founders and their wealth and business advisors have to think more creatively about possible pathways as they seek an exit.

Here are the scenarios we most commonly see when family business owners are contemplating the transition of a family business:

- The business owner is nearing retirement age.
- Succession issues are complicated (e.g., children not involved in the family business or capital needed to effectuate a succession plan).
- An unsolicited offer to buy the company has been received.
- There have been changes in the owner's health or marital status.
- The owner is motivated by news of a transaction involving a major competitor, customer or vendor.
- Regulatory issues from recent changes or enforcement have made a sale more attractive.

All of these scenarios have the potential to produce a great deal of uncertainty and apprehension. For founder-owners and families, it is often the most important financial decision of their lives. For advisors consulting with their business owner clients on the best path forward, there are four things they should encourage their clients to do before they even consider the possibility of a sale:

1. Get the Financials in Order

Buyers and their lenders evaluate financial statements in a very prescribed way. At minimum, business owners should have a full inventory of monthly income statements, a view of the balance sheet and statement of cash flows prepared in accordance with GAAP, utilizing the "accrual method" of accounting. Buyers will review financial statements and prepare their own analyses during due diligence. That's why presenting accurate financial statements is more important than whether they are currently audited, reviewed, compiled or internally generated.

2. Continue to Invest in the Business

Signaling to the buyer that the business has been properly reinvested in and maintained at the highest level is important. Though it's tempting to avoid making large capital expenditures in the years leading up to a sale, a business will fetch its highest valuation when properly capitalized and planning for future growth to allow the new buyer to execute its growth strategy without having to reduce the offer based on undercapitalized for growth. Similar to putting in a new kitchen when you sell the house, some improvements will increase more than 100% of your cost.

3. Create a Three-Year Forecast

Setting achievable goals and highlighting the company's competitive position will give buyers a better idea of how the company can grow and excel under their ownership. The projected numbers should be achievable in the proposed period. It is far better to be conservative in your projections, especially since some sales may be tied to future growth and results.

4. Focus on Sales and Growth

Any prospective buyer is going to look closely at the growth potential of the business. It makes strategic sense to work on growing sales efforts, which may mean hiring additional sales reps and increasing the overall investment in growth initiatives.

Most family-owned businesses are privately held partnerships or LLCs with single owner entities. Because entrepreneurs historically are laser-focused on building and running the business, founders are often less familiar with the details of their financials or what factors come into play in selling or merging a company. But by taking steps to get the business prepped for sale, and understanding what prospective buyers are looking for, they can increase their likelihood of a positive outcome.

In the end, it's all about helping the business owner and his or her family realize the greatest benefit, while giving them a sense of satisfaction that they've arrived at the right outcome.

When selling your Business, just as with your home or any large asset, you MUST prepare and have a plan, or you risk losing out on possible tax savings and ultimately how much is "left" in their pocket after taxes and closing costs.

Ultimately every business owner must answer three key questions:

1. How do I create and retain value in the business?
2. How do I attract and retain the "Key Employees " who will help me build this value?
3. How do I create an exit strategy so I can extract myself from this business and convert its fair market value (FMV) into retirement capital and income?

Creating and Retaining Value

The single biggest problem for most business owners is extracting and retaining money distributed from their company. There is a big difference between profit and personal income. During good times, owners often take out significant bonuses and dividend distributions. But when the economy tightens, they usually have to put money back into the company out of necessity. When the economy tightens, owners have few places to turn for business capital. As a result, business owners rarely have surplus capital outside of their business.

There are two common strategies for increasing owner wealth: Having a well-funded retirement plan or using an investment grade life insurance program. Most owners know how retirement plans work. But few owners know about how life insurance strategies can retain wealth and save taxes as well as be used for Key employees. These are specialty programs reserved just for owners and other highly compensated executives in lieu of stock. Unlike retirement plans, they don't have to be offered to all of your client's employees.

Retaining the Key Employees

Instead of giving away company stock, other options to consider are equity participation plans, or phantom stock plans, incentive stock plans or stock appreciation rights. Each plan allows the owner to allocate a certain number of shares (phantom shares) to a pool. The shares are then allocated each year based on a formula, and the shares are valued based on measurable metrics using earnings before interest, taxes, depreciation and amortization. But value could be based on increases in retained earnings or some multiplier of net profits.

Creating an Exit Strategy

With enough advance planning, owners should have several viable ways to exit their business. There are pros and cons, however, to each approach.

1. **Liquidate.** They could hold on to the business as long as possible and then just have the family liquidate the business by selling off all the assets at their death. It's usually a fire sale with no owner's goodwill. Valuable, income producing assets are sold at a substantial discount. Owners typically receive more for their business if sold as a going concern than if sold off piecemeal.

2. **Sell to an internal buyer.** Company insiders know the business well and will be motivated to sustain and grow it. The challenge is that most inside buyers—key employees—have no money to buy the company outright. So, owners must help them.

3. **Sell to an external buyer.** This is considered the holy grail of business succession, but even in good economic times it can be hard to find qualified buyers who will pay all cash all upfront without contingencies. Then there are capital gains taxes (roughly 25% federal, plus state taxes where applicable) and advisory fees, which can range from 4% to 8% of the selling price. After discounts, fees and taxes, owners must ask themselves: "Is the walkaway money enough to support the lifestyle I imagined for myself post-sale?"

Looking at just the finances of the sale

Let's consider selling your business. It's time and you have a fantastic offer. The buyer is willing to pay $15 million. Now how do you evaluate the offer? It can be hard to know if the offer is a good one. You decide not to sell because, based on projections, you can make more money in the short-term over the next five years than you were to sell the business. Don't forget when you sell a business you still have to pay off any debts and pay the taxes.

When an offer to buy is presented there are a lot of factors I work with my clients regarding selling. Is the money left over after debt and taxes put you in a position where you want to be? Many other questions are raised. For example, do you have family working in the business? Will they get fired or stay working? What about your other employees? How emotionally attached are you to the business?

So, the decision process has a lot to do with timing. The biggest question is; If you sell, what are you going to do?

It's very common that business owners sell one business in hopes of starting another. There are people who just have that knack. But there are others that don't know what they are going to do.

If the decision is made to sell the business, what does that look like?

If you chose to sell the business, then what? What are you going to do? Are you going to stay on in a consulting role? Are you going to just cash out, take your money and go?

If you chose to retire, then what?

Retirement, when it's forced or even planned, is never easy. Just like when you transition out of athletics into civilian life, if we want to call it that, it's still going to take three years, even though you planned well. *You should always start* a business with the exit strategy in mind. Things may change along the way and so will your plan.

CHAPTER 13

WHAT'S NEXT...

Let's talk a little about retirement. When someone reaches retirement age, hopefully they have financial resources prepared so they can stop working. Even if you have the financial structure, it is still a difficult transition. No different than your retirement from professional athletics, the journey of figuring out who you are and what you are going to do all day is not easy. *How are you going to prepare for it?*

Executives with public companies can amass a significant amount of cash for retirement. It may be $7 or 70 million. However, if they don't have a plan it can become unhealthy.

You can ask yourself, hey, *what do I really want to do? Do I have enough money to live off of? To never work again? Or just enough to survive before deciding on the next business or next adventure. Your health becomes important as well.* You want to make sure that you are both physically and mentally able.

This has a lot to do with who you are and your personal identity. What are your goals? It takes a lot of soul searching which is why you do not want to just stop without a plan. It is a thought process to put yourself in a position to make the transition easier and *plan* for it.

If you are going to retire as an athlete, you want to make sure that you have the financial ability to take some time to figure out what your next career may be. In some cases, you might have many ideas and you are ready to go. Make sure to take the time for preparation so you go into the game with the end result in mind and stick with the Game Plan.

THE NEW CORPORATE TRANSPARENCY ACT

New Federal Reporting Requirement for Beneficial Ownership Information (BOI) Effective January 1, 2024, many companies in the United States must report information about their beneficial owners—the individuals who ultimately own or control the company—to the Financial Crimes Enforcement Network (FinCEN), a bureau of the U.S. Department of the Treasury.

Who Has to Report?

While in some cases companies do not need to report, in general most every operating company must report. Companies required to report are called reporting companies. Reporting companies may have to obtain information from their beneficial owners and report that information to FinCEN.

Reporting companies report beneficial ownership information electronically through FinCEN's website: www.fincen.gov/boi. The system provides a confirmation of receipt once a completed report is filed with FinCEN.

When Do I Report?

FinCEN began accepting reports on January 1, 2024. • If your company was created or registered prior to January 1, 2024, you will have until January 1, 2025 to report BOI. • If your company is created or registered in 2024, you must report BOI within 90 calendar days after receiving actual or public notice that your company's creation or registration is effective, whichever is earlier. • If your company is created or registered on or after January 1, 2025, you must file BOI within 30 calendar days after receiving actual or public notice that its creation or registration is effective. • Any updates or corrections to beneficial ownership information that you previously filed with FinCEN must be submitted within 30 days

WHY are they doing this

The Financial Crimes Enforcement Network (FinCEN) issued a final rule implementing the bipartisan Corporate Transparency Act's (CTA) beneficial ownership information (BOI) reporting provisions. The rule will enhance the ability of FinCEN and other agencies to protect U.S. national security and the U.S. financial system from illicit use and provide essential information to national security, intelligence, and law enforcement agencies; state, local, and Tribal officials; and financial institutions to help prevent drug traffickers, fraudsters, corrupt actors such as oligarchs, and proliferators from laundering or hiding money and other assets in the United States.

Who Is a Beneficial Owner

- Under the rule, a beneficial owner includes any individual who, directly or indirectly, either (1) exercises substantial control over a reporting company, or (2) owns or controls at least 25 percent of the ownership interests of a reporting company. The rule defines the terms "substantial control" and "ownership interest." In keeping with the CTA, the rule exempts five types of individuals from the definition of "beneficial owner."

- In defining the contours of who has substantial control, the rule sets forth a range of activities that could constitute substantial control of a reporting company. This list captures anyone who is able to make important decisions on behalf of the entity. FinCEN's approach is designed to close loopholes that allow corporate structuring that obscures owners or decision-makers. This is crucial to unmasking anonymous shell companies.

- The rule provides standards and mechanisms for determining whether an individual owns or controls 25 percent of the ownership interests of a reporting company. Among other things, these standards and mechanisms address how a reporting company should handle a situation in which ownership interests are held in trust.

- These definitions have been drafted to account for the various ownership or control structures reporting companies may adopt. However, for reporting companies that have simple organizational structures it should be a straightforward process to identify and report their beneficial owners. FinCEN expects the majority of reporting companies will have simple ownership structures.

NOTE: Penalties include a $500 daily civil penalty, fines of up to $10,000 and a possible two-year prison sentence for those that do not provide or update beneficial ownership information with FinCEN.

APPENDIX II

STARTING A BUSINESS

How to Start a Business

- Is Entrepreneurship For You?
- 20 Questions Before Starting
- 10 Steps to Starting a Business

Understand Your Market

- Business Data & Statistics
- General Business Statistics
- Consumer Statistics
- Demographics
- Economic Indicators
- Employment Statistics
- Income Statistics
- Money & Interest Rates
- Production & Sales Statistics
- Trade Statistics
- Statistics for Specific Industries

Business Types

- Green Businesses
- Startups & High Growth Businesses
- Home-Based Businesses
- Online Businesses
- Franchise Businesses
- Buying Existing Businesses
- Self Employed & Independent Contractors
- Women-Owned Businesses
- Veteran-Owned Businesses
- People with Disabilities
- Young Entrepreneurs
- Encore Entrepreneurs
- Minority-Owned Businesses
- Native Americans

Find a Mentor or Counselor
Write Your Business Plan

- Executive Summary
- Company Description
- Market Analysis
- Organization & Management
- Service or Product Line
- Marketing & Sales
- Funding Request
- Financial Projections
- Appendix
- How to Make Your Business Plan Stand Out

Choose Your Business Structure

- Sole Proprietorship
- Limited Liability Company
- Cooperative
- Corporation
- Partnership
- S Corporation

Choose & Register Your Business

- Choose Your Business Name
- Register Your Business Name
- Register With State Agencies

Choose Your Business Location & Equipment
Tips for Choosing Your Business Location

- Basic Zoning Laws
- Home-Based Business Zoning Laws
- Leasing Commercial Space
- Buying Government Surplus
- Leasing Business Equipment

Business Licenses & Permits

- Federal Licenses & Permits
- State Licenses & Permits

Learn About Business Laws

- Advertising & Marketing Law
- Employment & Labor Law

- Finance Law
- Intellectual Property Law

Online Business Law

- Collecting Sales Tax Online
- International Online Sales

Privacy Law

- Environmental Regulations
- Regulation of Financial Contracts
- Workplace Safety & Health Law
- Foreign Workers & Employee Eligibility

Contact a Government Agency

- Assistance with Regulatory Compliance
- Economic Development Agencies

Business Financials

- Estimating Startup Costs
- Using Personal Finances
- Preparing Financial Statements
- Developing a Cash Flow Analysis
- Break Even Analysis
- Borrowing Money for Your Business
- Is Your Business Fiscally Fit?

Finance Your Business
Loans

- SBA Loans
- Business Loan Application Checklist
- SBA Loan Application Checklist
- Acquiring Financing

Grants
Venture Capital

- Venture Capital
- SBIC Directory

Business USA Financing Tool
Filing & Paying Taxes

- Is It A Business or a Hobby?
- Obtain Your Federal Business Tax ID
- Determine Your Federal Tax Obligations
- Determine Your State Tax Obligations
- Determine When the Tax Year Starts

Hire & Retain Employees

APPENDIX III

MENTORSHIP

Excerpts from thebalancesmb.com "the value of a business-mentor" (Allen/2018) and Virgin. com's "10 tips to becoming perfect business mentor"

Learn Why Every Entrepreneur Should Have a Business Mentor

Your friends and family, the online gurus, publications, and even casual acquaintances can provide you with a steady flow of information regarding news, industry developments, and opportunities. Industry analysts, consultants, employees, and good networking contacts can share their expert knowledge with you regarding particular situations and needs you may encounter. However, only a business mentor can truly share wisdom with you on an ongoing basis, and in a manner that can have a direct positive impact on the growth of your business over time.

The generic business advice you'll get from online publications will only go so far, and a good business mentor picks up right where that leaves off.

A business mentor is someone with more entrepreneurial business experience than you, who serves as a trusted confidante over an extended period of time, usually free of charge.

Does this sound a little too good to be true? Well, first and foremost, being a business mentor to an up-and-coming entrepreneur is a great way of giving back to their community, and to society at large when their advice and guidance can have a measurable impact helping their mentees.

Many business mentors may advise people in order to develop their skills as a teacher, man- ager, strategist, or consultant. Moreover, a true mentorship relationship also works in both directions—your mentor gets to learn about new ideas, strategies and tactics from you, just as you'll learn timeless wisdom from them.

Here are five key benefits of finding a business mentor:

Where else are you going to turn?

Once you launch into your own business, there's no boss to turn to for advice or direction when you're in a pinch—maybe not even any employees yet. Although you're flying solo, you don't have to be. Everybody needs a good reliable sounding board, second opinion, and sometimes just emotional support when the times get tough (which they will).

1. They've "been there and done that".

   Perhaps the most obvious benefit of finding a business mentor is that you can learn from their previous mis- takes and successes. Your mentor doesn't need to have experience in your particular industry—though it helps if they do—so that you're maximizing your opportunities to leverage key relationships. They don't have to be up on the latest trends or technology—you've got other sources for that. Your mentor's role is to share with you lessons from their experience in the hopes that you can learn them quickly and easily.

2. It's (usually) free.

   If you're on a tight budget, that's a major fac- tor. While good coaches and consultants may be able to offer some things that a mentor doesn't, it almost always comes at a price, usually of several hundred dollars (or more) each month. Mentors, though, are readily available, free of charge through a number of organizations, such as SCORE (Service Corps of Retired Executives) and many other groups. Plan on at least treating your mentor to lunch or coffee when you meet together.

3. Expand your social network.

   Your mentor, being an experienced businessperson, is likely to have an extensive network, and can offer you access to far more senior decision- makers than you cur- rently have. They will be far more willing to open that network up to you than some casual acquaintance from a networking meeting.

4. A trusted, long-term relationship.

   Your mentor has no ulterior motive—no service or prod- uct to sell you. That, combined with their experience, cre- ates a good foundation for trust. And as the relationship develops over time, that trust can grow even stronger. Also, your time with them becomes more and more effi- cient as they become more and more familiar with you and your business.

As you can see, the rewards are potentially great to bring on a business mentor, and the risk is non-existent. You have nothing to lose and everything to gain by finding a good mentor. Every entrepreneur should have one.

There's a decline in the number of businesses starting up in the United States as we see the economy improving. This means less people are starting businesses out of necessity, and instead people are doing so out of passion and because they see an opportunity in the market.

Programs like The Presidential Ambassadors for Global Entrepreneurship are focused on devel- oping the next generation of entrepreneurs, but what can we individually do to help? You may know someone who is interested in starting their own business or embodies the entrepreneurial spirit – perhaps an intern or employee at your company, your neighbor, maybe even your child. Here are some suggestions on how to work with the next generation to set them up for success as a business owner.

While starting a business out of passion rather than necessity sets one up for success initially, the fact remains that many entrepreneurs lack the basic business or leadership skills that are necessary to maintain or grow a business. We see new businesses fail all the time, and the majority of the time it's due to incompetence.

1. Communication – Being able to communicate effectively will help build relationships, problem solve, and convey what a business is and why consumers need whatever is being sold. Unfortunately, many young people are lacking at face-to-face interactions because of social media and text messages. Successful businesses require that people actually speak to one another.

   Start with the importance of a professional appearance and introductions (eye contact, hand- shake) and the importance of the elevator speech. As an entrepreneur, they'll likely have to pitch their business and it's got to be on point in order to compete.

2. Leadership – Look for opportunities to put them in charge. The bottom line is that an entrepreneur is their own boss, and might eventually be the manager of other people. They need to have experience taking ownership of things and making decisions.

   Goal setting – Have a conversation to under- stand what the individual aspires to be. Jot down several goals and have them pick the one that makes the most sense to be their main focus. Figure out what steps are necessary to accomplish this goal and encourage them to start taking action on those steps immediately. Remember, goals can be altered and now's the perfect time to lay some ground-work for a future business.

3. Recognize opportunities – Teaching future entrepreneurs to seek out opportunities and act on them will directly contribute to their level of future success. Encourage young people to point out small problems or setbacks in their lives or at work. Brainstorm solutions on how to resolve their troubles. This will teach them to focus on creating positive solutions, instead of focusing on the problem itself.

4. Failure – we're often taught that failure is unacceptable. When it comes to entrepreneur-ship, failure can be a positive thing if there is a lesson learned. Budding entrepreneurs need to understand that at some point, something is not going to go their way – it's part of owning a business.

5. It's important to be resilient and learn from the situation so they grow as an individual and make better business decisions in the future.

6. Giving back – Every entrepreneur hopes to be successful one day. Understanding the importance of giving back will help the next generation stay humble during periods

of success and it will teach them that a successful business provides benefits to more than just its owner.

7. Independence – Having the freedom to make your own decisions is often considered to be one of the greatest benefits of entrepreneurship. The key to independence is confidence. In many cases, confidence must be learned. In the case of a future entrepreneur, they're going to learn to believe in their own abilities from acting on challenges, seeing the results and being praised and respected by others.

8. Financial literacy – This is one area where entrepreneurs really struggle. It's one thing to manage your own bank account, but what about managing the money coming in and out of a business? At work, let an aspiring entrepreneur co- own the department's budget. It's also a good idea to prep them for the fact that they will likely need help in this area; an accountant can serve as an advisor on where a business's money is going vs. where it should be going.

APPENDIX IV

MONEY AND CREDIT

Why Budget?

- Helps you to live within your means and meet expenses
- Helps you save for long- and short-term goals
- Giving you goals to achieve and monitor

Why Save?

- In case of an emergency
- To take advantage of opportunities
- To reach financial goals

The Debit Card

- ATM Card bit with Bank logo
- Looks just like a credit card, but not a loan, no interest
- Backed only by the checking account behind it
- Widely accepted, can be a good budgeting tool
- Immediate use of money, make sure you don't go overdraft.

When to Use Debit Card vs Credit Card vs Cash

How you spend money for everyday expenses like groceries, gas, movie theaters and restaurants, clothing should be part of an "overall" spending and savings plan to keep you on track.

Your Credit Score

- Everything you do with your credit accounts affects your credit score including car and school loan
- Creditors extend credit to credit worthy customers
- When you pay your bills on time, you are proving yourself credit worthy
- Banks reward good customers with lower interest rate loans and higher credit lines
- Employers may check your score. A bad score may result in fewer job offers
- Non-installment credit
  - Regular
  - 30-day charge accounts (American Express)
  - Travel and entertainment cards
- Installment credit
  - Car loan, student loan, home loan
  - Furniture purchase
- Revolving credit
  - Department store cards
  - Bank cards: Visa/MasterCard

THREE factors that your Credit Score Says about you

Character – how well you handle financial obligations

Capital – the assets you own, including real estate, savings and investments

Capacity – how much debt you can man- age based upon your income

Character

Character is an evaluation of how likely you are to repay your debts. Potential lenders look at your past history, including:

- How well you've handled your money in the past.
- Did you pay bills on time?
- Have you ever filed for bankruptcy?
- How long have you lived at your present address?
- How long have you been at your present job?

Capacity

Capacity looks at how much debt you can handle based on your current financial situation. Lenders want to know whether or not you have been working regularly in a job that will provide enough income to support your credit use.

- Do you have a steady job or income?
- How much do you earn?
- How many other loan payments do you have?
- What are your current living expenses?
- What other debts do you have?
- Do you have children or other dependents that you are supporting?

Advantages of being creditworthy:

- You are more likely to secure favorable rates on loans and credit accounts
- You may qualify for lower auto insurance rates
- You will be able to open utility accounts for your apartment or house without paying large deposits

Challenges of NOT being considered creditworthy:

- You will not be able to get loans or credit cards
- You will be charged higher loan and credit card interest rates
- You may be rejected in favor of candidates with better credit histories when you apply to rent an apartment

APPENDIX V

THE POWER OF SAVING

1. Simple interest

Principal x interest rate x time = interest earned

$100,000 x .05 x 1 = $5000 interest earned every year

2. Compound interest

When your interest compounds, it gets added back to your account and becomes part of your principal. With more principal, the account earns even more interest, which continually compounds into new principal. It's a powerful cycle that really adds up.

In the simple interest example above,

$100,000 at a 5% simple APR, earns $5000 in interest every year.

However, if that interest compounds once a year, the $5000 interest you earn in year one would be added to the principal at the beginning of year two. By doing this, you earn more interest in year two ($5,250.) and even more in every subsequent year.

$100,000 x .05 x 1 = $5000 interest earned in year one

$100,050 x .05 x 1 = $5250 interest earned in year two

3. The Rule of 72 – Double Down

How fast can your money DOUBLE? The Rule of 72 is a fast way to estimate how long it will take you to double your savings with com- pound interest. How it is calculated:

72 divided by the interest rate = the number of years needed to double your money. Therefore, if you have a 10% interest rate and want to know how long it will take to double your money, the equation would be:

72 divided by 10 = 7.2 years

APPENDIX VI

ADVISORS

1. Lawyer (JD)
   o Estate Planning- protection for Probate, Creditors, execute your wishes
   o Asset Protection – protection from Creditors
   o Litigation – You sue someone or someone sues you
   o Intellectual Property – setup and protect your brand
   o Business Attorney – regular operations of a business, documents and compliance with state and federal laws

   American Bar Association Service Center – to find your local state bar (800) 285-2221

   [International (312) 988-5000]

   https://www.americanbar.org/about_the_aba/ contact/

2. Investment Advisor (CFP, ChFA, etc)
   o Choosing the right investments
   o Education you on what you are investing in and why
   o Planning for Long Term and Short Term
   o May also help with

- o Life Insurance

- o Disability Insurance

- o Long Term Care Insurance

3. Certified Public Accountant (CPA)
   - o Taxes, Taxes and more Taxes

   - o Business Structure

   - o Business Plan development

   - o Business management

   - o Personal CFO

   - o Business Consulting and Planning

NASBA – National Associations of the State Board Of Accountants

To find your local state board https://nasba.org/ 150 Fourth Ave. North, Ste. 700

Nashville, TN 37219-2417

Phone: (615) 880-4200

APPENDIX VII

GOAL SETTING

Before the start of the season, before the start of any game, before the start of an athletic career, you set goals. Win the Stanley Cup, Super Bowl, World Series, NBA champs, Gold Medals or NCAA Championships, those are goals! They are concrete and the path to achieving them is pretty straight forward. Those are team goals. While the Olympics may be individual goals, it still resonates as a goal for the Olympic Team or your Country. Individual goals may be a number of Wins, Hits, Goals, Touchdowns, etc.

Goals for professionals, entrepreneurs, or employees may be slightly less concrete or the path may be indirect. If your goal is to be the CFO of a Publicly Traded company, that is a lofty and achievable goal; however, the path to get there may be direct or may take thousands of little goals.

What about FINANCIAL GOALS?

Basic financial goals revolve around money. Getting it (Earnings), Keeping it (Saving), using it wisely (Budgets), growing it (investments) or giving it away (Charity.) Any way you want to set your goals there is no right or wrong answer.

How to set your goals is up to you. Who helps you process your desires and wishes, who helps you achieve them, what they are, is ALL up to you.

Once you set your goals, how you get there is the challenge. Start by working backward. If your goal is to hit .300 in baseball, then start with what is my batting average today. Next, you need to consult with experts on how to improve your bat- ting stance, swing, mental approach to the plate, how you perform against certain teams, pitchers, stadiums, weather etc.

Harvey Mackay recently published an article in his syndicated column that 'Goals require growth to be achieved." He has his own formula for goals.

- Make it Positive - don't set your goal to be "not to strike out so much."
- Be fully Committed.
- Step By Step – By working with your professional team, you can build a program to reach your goals. I recently sat with my investment advisor and said; "this is what I want to have when I retire, here is where I am now, how do I get there?" We then set up a 10-year plan to achieve the goal.
- Appreciate the learning experience – you may have challenges and delays or other hurdles in front of you. Figure out what does NOT work, what DOES work and why.
- Take them seriously – if you don't, no one else will either.
- Trust your judgment - In addition trust the judgment of your professional advisors/ coaches. There is NO rule against asking for help.

- BE AMBITIOUS - there is no sense in achieving a goal that does not require effort, if it seems too big, then break it up into smaller goals along your path.

Mackay's Moral: Don't be afraid to dream big – be afraid not to.

APPENDIX VIII

LARGE ASSET PURCHASES – CARS AND HOMES (SOURCE VISA FINANCIAL SOCCER, 2012,2018)

I did not want to overload you with too much information, so I wanted to make sure you knew how complicated and how intricate the two largest purchases you may make in your life can be.

When shopping for a car

1. Decisions
   - Deciding how much to spend (Need vs Wants)
   - How to Pay for it All Cash or Car Loan
   - Do I get New or Used?
   - How do I Finance it? Lease or Purchase

2. Private Party or Dealer or Carvana online
   If you decide on a used car from a dealer
   - Consider costs, reliability, dealer reputation
   - Research Carfax, Edmunds, KBB etc.

3. Consider the warranty and the service contract
   - What to do if you have problems
   - A used car from a private party
   - Sometimes includes a manufacturer's warranty
   - Difference in price compared to a dealer

4. A new car
   - Read about new car features and prices
   - Shop around
   - Plan to negotiate price
   - Learn the terms
   - Consider the service contract

Car Loans

What to consider when shopping for a car loan

- Annual Percentage Rate of Interest
- Length of loan
- Monthly payments
- Total finance charge
- Total to be repaid
- Shop around for a car loan and compare the Interest Rate
- What is a Lease? How is it different from a Loan/ Purchase?
- What is a co-signer?
- Understand the circumstances under which a vehicle can be repossessed, and list the legal
- Rights and responsibilities of the creditor and of the debtor

The cost to own, operate, and maintain a car
- Initial purchase price
- Registration and title costs
- Sales tax
- Financing cost
- Insurance
- Scheduled maintenance
- Unscheduled repairs and maintenance
- Gasoline, oil and other fluids
- Parking and tolls

About warranties and service contracts
1. Types of warranties
   - As-is warranty
   - Implied warranty
   - Dealer warranty
   - Manufacturer's warranty
2. Service contracts
3. Preventing problems
4. Resolving disputes
5. Comparing promises of warranties and service contract

About auto insurance
1. Importance of and legal requirements
2. Types of coverage
   - Bodily injury liability
   - Property damage liability
   - Collision

- o Comprehensive
- o Medical payments
- o Uninsured motorist
- o Rental reimbursement
- o Towing and labor

3. How insurance rates are set
   - o Age
   - o Sex
   - o Marital status
   - o Personal habits (e.g., smoking)
   - o Type of use
   - o Frequency of use
   - o Location
   - o Driving record deductible
   - o Type of car
   - o Value and age of car

BUYING A HOME

First, SHOULD I buy or Rent Comparing renting and buying

1. Main advantages of renting are:
   - o Ease of mobility – Lock it and Leave it
   - o Fewer responsibilities
   - o Lower initial costs – no cost for repairs and Maintenance

2. Common disadvantages of renting are:
   - Few financial benefits in the form of tax deductions
   - Restricted lifestyle, decorating, having pets, and other activities
   - Legal concerns (landlords and neighbors)
   - No opportunity to have the value of a home

3. Key benefits of buying your housing are:
   - Tax savings
   - Pride of ownership
   - Potential economic gain

4. Disadvantages of buying your house may include:
   - Financial risks related to having down payment funds, obtaining a mortgage, fluctuating
   - property values
   - Limited mobility if a home is difficult to sell
   - Higher living costs due to repairs and maintenance

BUYING A HOME, The process

1. Phase 1 - How much home do you NEED vs WANT
2. Phase 2 - Location Location Location
3. Phase 3 - Finding a home within your Price
4. Phase 4 - Finance and Close
   - Applying for a mortgage
     - ✦ Determine an estimated value of the house
     - ✦ Obtain funds for a down payment
     - ✦ Know your credit score

- ✦ Compare fees, services, and mortgage rates for different lenders
- ○ Prepare the mortgage application
  - ✦ types of mortgages
  - ✦ A conventional mortgage has equal payments, typically over 15, 30, or 40 years based on a fixed interest rate
  - ✦ Government-guaranteed financing pro- grams include loans from the Federal Housing Authority (FHA) and the Veterans Administration (VA)
  - ✦ A balloon mortgage has fixed monthly payments and a very large final payment, usually after three, five, or seven years
  - ✦ The adjustable rate mortgage (ARM), also referred to as a flexible rate mort- gage or a variable rate mortgage, has an interest rate that increases or decreases during the life of the loan based on changes in market interest rates
  - ✦ A graduated payment mortgage has payments rising to different levels during the term of the loan
  - ✦ An interest-only mortgage consists of interest-only payments for a specified period, usually five to ten years
  - ✦ Reverse mortgages provide an elderly homeowner with tax-free income in the form of a loan that is paid back (with interest) when the home is sold or the homeowner dies
  - ✦ Refinancing refers to obtaining a new mortgage on your current home at a lower interest rate

○ Selecting a mortgage

✦ Shop around for mortgages through multiple lenders

✦ Estimate a mortgage payment based on different factors including interest rates and different terms of the loan closing costs

○ The common costs associated with the settlement of a real estate transaction may include:

✦ Attorney or escrow fees

✦ Title insurance

✦ Property taxes

✦ Appraisal fee

✦ Recording fees, transfer taxes

✦ Loan discount points

✦ Inspections

✦ Lender's origination fee

✦ Reserves for home insurance and property taxes

✦ Interest (paid from date of closing to 30 days before first monthly payment)

✦ Real estate agent commission

BIBLIOGRAPHY

Motley Fool.com; 6 Financial Mistakes That Are Ruining Your Credit; Kailey Fralick Jul 23; https://www.fool.com/credit-cards/2018/07/23/6-financial-mistakes-that-are-ruining-your-credit.aspx

Motley Fool.com; 3 Smart Ways to Save Money on Your Next Car; Matthew Frankel, CFP ; Sep 13, 2018; https://www.fool.com/ retirement/2018/09/13/3-smart-ways-to- save-money-on-your-next-car.aspx

Investopedia.com; what is a Budget? Budgeting Terms and Tips; Reviewed by Julia Kagen ; Updated Jan 17, 2018; https://www.investopedia.com/terms/b/budget.asp

Investopedia.com; How to Find a Financial Advisor/Planner ; https://www.investopedia.com/updates/find-financial-advisor-planner.

Investopedia.com; https://www.investopedia. com/financial-edge/0312/why-athletes-go-broke.aspx; Why Athletes Go Broke ; Tim Parker ; Mar 5, 2012

Nerdwallet; Associated Press Former stars explain why NFL players go broke, and what you can learn;; Oct. 10, 2017 https:// www.businessinsider.com/ap-liz-weston- why-nfl-players-go-broke-and-what-you- can-learn-2017-10

Investopedia.com; What do Financial Advisors Do; https:// www.investopedia.com/articles/personal-finance/050815/ what- do-financial-advisers-do.asp

https://www.pressreader.com/usa/the-arizona-republic/20181 224/281621011449525 Dec 24, 2018 - Goals require growth to be achieved

Investopedia.com Risk Tolerance; https://www. investopedia. com/articles/pf/07/risk_tolerance.asp

Motley Fool.com; Budgeting 101: How to Start Budgeting for the First Time; Christy

Bieber; Apr 21, 2018 at 10:16AM; https:// www.fool.com/ investing/2018/04/21/budgeting-101-how-to-start-budgeting-for-the-first.aspx?source=isesitlnk0000001 &mrr=1.00

Pacific Standard Magazine; How We Set Up Our Professional Athletes to Fail; Author: Sam Riches; Publish date:Feb 18, 2014 https:// psmag.com/economics/professional - athletes-set-fail-74247

Forbes.com; Curt Schilling And Why Athletes Make Such Poor Financial Decisions; Monte Burke ; SportsMoney; May 25, 2012, 12:50pm; https://www.forbes.com/ sites/ monteburke/2012/05/25/curt- schilling-and-why-athletes-make-such- poor-financial-decisions/#12ddfb9531b4

American Psychological Association; Exercise and Sport Psychology Newsletter; May 2016; https://www.apa.org/ about/division/ div47.aspx

Floyd Little, Interview for "Beyond the Game", (Silverlight Films, 2017)

Securities and Exchange Commission; SEC.gov https://www. investor.gov/research-before-you-invest/research/ five-questions-ask-before-you-invest

By Kareem Abdul-Jabbar; 20 Things I Wish I'd Known When I Was 30; When I was thirty, Apr 30, 2013; https://www.esquire.com/news-politics/news/a22394/ kareem- things-i-wish-i-knew/

Paychex Inc; https://www.paychex.com/articles/ startup/ employee-to-entrepreneur-businesses-start;

NCAA, http://www.ncaa.org/about/resources/ research/ estimated-probability-competing-college-athletics; 2018

https://www.thebalancesmb.com/the-value-of-a- business-mentor-1200818 (Allen/2018)

NCAA; http://www.ncaa.org/about/resources/ research/ estimated-probability-competing-professional-athletics; 2018

Michelle Gill; Value of and contributions of the participation in intercollegiate athletics on the personal development of communitycollege-aged students; (2015) http:// digitalcommons.unl.edu/cehsedaddiss/232

Pro Athletes Prove Why You Should Stick To A Financial Playbook; Aug 16, 2017, Zach Conway https://www.forbes. com/sites/ zachconway/2017/08/16/pro-athletes- prove-why-you-should-stick-to-a-financial- playbook/ college-aged students; (2015) http://digitalcommons.unl.edu/ cehsedaddiss/232

Danny Schayes; Fast Broke: Learn the reason athletes go broke; Nomad CEO Publishing; isbn 13: 978-1502869715.

https://www.virgin.com/entrepreneur/10-tips-becoming-perfect-business-mentor

https://www.sba.gov/business-guide/

Money 101; Visa Practical Money Skills; https://www.practical moneyskills.com; (2018)

Robert Pagliarini ; Why athletes go broke: The myth of the dumb jock; MoneyWatch; https://www.cbsnews.com/news/why-athletes-go-broke-the-myth-of-the-dumb-jock; (2013)

Jonathan Miller CPA; https://www.forbes.com; want-to-retire-early-take-a-cue-from-the-pro-baller-playbook. (2016)

Jonathan Miller, CPA; https://www.cnbc.con; for-athletes-like-sergio-garcia-tax-season-brings-extra-burdens (2017)

Jonathan Miller, CPA; NFL Rookie year; Life after football; Interview WBEZ; (2015) http://www.sportsfinancial.org/nfl-rookie- yearlife-after-football-wbezs-morning-shift/

Jonathan Miller, CPA; Professional Athletes Retirement Conundrum; Chief Investment Officer Magazine; http://www.ai-ciodigital. com/ai-cio; (2016)

Susan Johnson Taylor; interview with Jonathan Miller , CPA; https://money.usnews.com/money/personal-finance/articles; (2016)22/what-pro-athletes-can-teach-us-about-retirement-planning

Amy Armstrong; The Suit Magazine; Don't Blow It; interview with Jonathan Miller, CPA (2016)

Jonathan Miller, CPA; Wall Street Journal on Advising Professional Athletes; https://www.wsj.com/articles/SB1000142412788 7323419604578573341985977374 via @ WSJ.

https://www.cnbc.com/2015/04/23/maybe-floyd-mayweathers-spending-is-the-key-to-winning.html Maybe Floyd Mayweather's spending is the key to winning; Robert Frank (2015)

Sheth, Hela & M. Babiak, Kathy. (2010). Beyond the Game: Perceptions and Practices of Corporate Social Responsibility in the Professional Sport Industry. Journal of Business Ethics. 91. 433-450. 10.1007/s10551-009-0094-0. (2010)

Babiak, Kathy & Mills, Brian & Tainsky, Scott & Juravich, Matthew. (2012). An Investigation Into Professional Athlete Philanthropy: www.growingagreenerworld.com/jason-brown-football-player-to-farmer/2019 https://www.sec.gov/litigation/ admin/2017/34-79991.pdf

AUTHOR BIO

Jonathan Miller, a native of Los Angeles, CA, currently resides in Paradise Valley, AZ. He has over 30 years of experience as a Certified Public Accountant in business and tax services. Through his consulting services, Jonathan is able to integrate his four core capabilities: strategic business planning, corporate structure, tax planning, and compliance to provide you or your business with solutions that fit your specific needs. Jonathan is also experienced working with CEO's, Professional Athletes and Entertainers as a Business Manager.

Jonathan founded StarCross Management LLC to serve his clients in the Sports and Entertainment Industry and has extensive experience in the Music and Publishing industry, including working with local start up bands as well as establish artists as well as Professional Athletes in the NHL, NFL, NBA and MLB including some international athletes in Soccer (football), UFC and the Olympics. Most recently Jonathan and his team have created a program for the collegiate athletes and NIL contracts in the multiple millions of dollars. His book, "Wait Don't Sign that NIL Contract" has been distributed to colleges across the country. Currently his book is being used as an integral tool for the college tour of "Beyond the Game", a film co-produced by Jonathan and Susan Sember through Silverlight Films that documents the financial journey of many former athletes.

Over the past 30 years Jonathan's commitment to healthcare has grown as the economic changes have forced physicians to look past their primary objective, that of providing care, to that of earning a living.

Jonathan's years of experience have led to the belief that he and his team of professionals can make a difference in the financial lives of their clients be they Doctors, Lawyers, Entrepreneurs or Professional Athletes.

Jonathan Miller CPA
President and Shareholder, Jonathan Miller, CPA, PC
Founder and Managing Member, Starcross Management, LLC
Co-Founder, Sports Financial Advisors Association
Founder, The Just 1 Project

www.ingramcontent.com/pod-product-compliance
Lightning Source LLC
Chambersburg PA
CBHW022339280326
41934CB00006B/695